# Trickster Tactics

A Festschrift in Honor of
Peter Nazareth

# TRICKSTER TACTICS

## A Festschrift in Honor of Peter Nazareth

Edited by S. G. Ellerhoff

Goa 1556

2021

*Trickster Tactics – A Festschrift Honoring Peter Nazareth*
Edited by S. G. Ellerhoff stevegronertellerhoff@gmail.com
Published by

Goa 1556

ISBN: 9788194963257

*For Peter & Mary*

## ACKNOWLEDGMENTS

Deep gratitude to Frederick Noronha, who graciously supported this tribute to Peter Nazareth from the outset. Thank you for publishing our blessings to a luminary who has changed so many of our lives for the better. Goa 1556's publication of several of Nazareth's works prior to this volume set the tenor when I sought a publisher. Your help along the way has been wonderful.

Praise for Mary Nazareth, who, among other magic, helped me orchestrate this behind Peter's back. Special thanks go to Peter and Mary's daughters, Monique and Kathy, for so many reasons. On a personal note, I am grateful to them for help they gave me when, at the start of the COVID-19 pandemic, I suddenly lost both of my jobs. The kindness you extended will always be remembered.

Thanks also to Michelle Van Ness, a former student of Nazareth's, who painted the mercurial image on the cover of this book as part of her final project for his course on African Literature. Anyone who visited Peter in his office will recognize it immediately. Thank you for this astonishing image. On that note, many thanks also to John Lyons and Hannah Sorrell, who work the front desk of the English Department at the University of Iowa. During the 2020 pandemic, they got into Peter's office and took the photo of the painting for the front cover.

I wish to thank Philip Coleman, too, for some helpful pointers on organizing the Festschrift.

I very warmly extend joy and gratitude to each of our contributors, who so graciously added their ingredients to the finished gumbo you hold in your hands. Thank you for making this happen!

S. G. Ellerhoff

# CONTENTS

# AN INTRODUCTION TO OUR GUMBO YA-YA

I heard of Professor Nazareth before I met him. He is that sort of professor, reputation preceding him. My mother was a high school English teacher and Julie Markussen was her student teacher during my first year of college. It was Julie who urged me to take Professor Nazareth's class on Elvis Presley. The way she sold it is very much the way I have since heard people in Ireland speak of John Moriarty, a twenty-first-century philosopher from Kerry who was commonly known on his part of the island as the local wise man. Nazareth knew things about Elvis, taught things about Elvis—if there was one class I had to take at the University of Iowa, it was the one he taught on Elvis.

At nineteen, I was less than lukewarm on Presley. I adhered to the lie perpetrated in outtakes from Quentin Tarantino's *Pulp Fiction* that you are either a Beatles person or an Elvis person. The Beatles provided my teenaged musical keystone, despite my being a generation removed from them. John Lennon was a hero to me. And Elvis had been a musical hero to him; of him, Lennon said, "Without Elvis there would be no Beatles" (qtd. in Sheff 86). That connection coaxed me toward enrolling in Nazareth's course, but Julie's fervor was most convincing. I signed up the second semester of my sophomore year—spring of the year 2000—and found there a deep appreciation Elvis Presley's artistry, for my culture's musical heritage, and—most importantly—a mentor.

Nazareth is utterly unique, unlike anyone I will ever know. I, a white, middle-class undergraduate from Des Moines, had been struggling personally at the mostly white, mostly middle-class University of Iowa. The school was huge. The professors distant. I felt out of place, had failed the first year and a half to make the sorts of connections college is supposedly all about. But then something ignited in Nazareth's course. Here was a personable, great-humored professor who thrived off direct interactions with the students arrayed before him. A Goan intellectual and literary artist born and raised in Uganda, his life, his experiences, his perspectives were of a quality I could not have found in anyone else—not just in landlocked Iowa, but in the world. For someone like me, coming from a white-collar Midwestern town, Nazareth brought a sophisticated and kindly exposure to the great wide world beyond. He also delivered concepts and points of view (plural!) on American arts and life that I could not come to on my own because I was so very much a product of the American system.

In front of a class of thirty, the good professor—often wearing a bolo tie—lectured on threads of songs, keeping dialogue going with the students and playing the music for us on a portable boombox. From a mysterious address book kept in his suit jacket, he would write the song titles, singers' names, their years of birth and death, and the years of the recordings in chalk on the blackboard. Sometimes the threads were of much earlier recordings, flowing into Elvis's versions. Sometimes they started with an Elvis song and then moved on to recordings of that song by others. Some classes we were listening to earlier artists, then Elvis, then later artists singing the same song. What we received was a sprawling sense of the unending dialogue at work in twentieth-century popular music. Suddenly all of the singers were heard to be communicating with one another. The lodestar was Elvis, but the hundreds of musicians we listened to were connected to him and his work.

That is where the course's title came from. As Nazareth explains it, "I called it Elvis As Anthology. You imagine a book called *Elvis*. You open it, inside you find Mario Lanza, Bing

Crosby, Little Richard, and so on. Why? Because Elvis was a twin whose twin brother was born dead, and he was always twinning himself to other people" (qtd. in thelibrarychannel). Few of us who are scholars can distill our work or a course we teach to such a concentrated and understandable thesis. I love the humanity of the idea, the way the artist's psychobiography is taken into account. It casts Elvis as an unusually talented person who was brought up with loss from the beginning, someone who sought the deep connection of intimacy with others through artistic means. Nazareth's reading of Elvis appeals to the best in all of us.

But that explanation is only part of the story. Elvis As Anthology is also the idea that whoever or whatever we decide Elvis is, he both contains and expresses multitudes through performance in music and film. This is still a revolutionary idea. Many people in America prefer to see in Elvis a foolish, uneducated, handsome (until the year or two before he died) southerner lacking any kind of comprehensive understanding of his own success, condemning the sounds he made to the dumb luck of a working-class rube with the biggest record labels and film studios behind him. The prejudice—and ignorance—directed toward Presley runs thick. And yet, as Nazareth shows us again and again, Elvis breaks through. Once we start paying attention, we cannot deny that Presley was an artist for the ages, utterly serious and accomplished in his craft. Cynics point to his decline in his final years, often with body shame; rarely do they know that his vocals on the last two LPs are more virtuosic than anything else he recorded. Listen to "Hurt," bellowed at Graceland in the Jungle Room. Listen to his solo piano recording, on the road his final year, of "Unchained Melody." Writing Elvis off ultimately says more about us than it does about him, especially once we realize that Presley was pouring himself into his art to the very end, affecting people deeply around the world and, now more than forty years later, across time.

Where did I learn this way of appreciating an artist I had foolishly written off? From Peter Nazareth.

***

Professor Nazareth, unlike a lot of professors, faithfully kept office hours. I started pestering him, showing up so I could ask him more questions about Elvis. What happened though, from my very first visit, was hearing about everything else on top of Elvis. Nazareth will joke about how talkative he was as a child, to the point where his parents would have him go talk to the cook. As a student, I benefited from his way of conversation, drawing lines across fields and artforms to discuss the most significant aspects of being alive. He could connect Elvis to Paramahansa Yogananda to Robert Anton Wilson to D. H. Lawrence to Alice Walker to Ishmael Reed to Bessie Head and then back to Elvis. He spoke of so many things, openly sharing his experiences in Uganda, in postgraduate school in England, in his professional life and the path to professorship. The visits deepened my sense of living and forged a strong friendship. Nazareth's acrobatics, rooted in intuition and intercomnect-edness, modeled for me the way a life spent studying and creating literature can temper one's consciousness. Julie had said his class would blow my mind—but the pedagogical relationship that took root did far more than that. It changed the way my mind worked. And lucky for me, the gracious professor never reacted unfavorably to finding me sitting on the floor outside his office, waiting for him to arrive. He would simply unlock his door and invite me in for a chat until another student showed up. He accepted me and my desire to learn.

The following winter, one of those catastrophes that befall

homeowners happened to the Nazareths: a burst pipe. Peter and Mary lived in a hotel for half a year while their house was repaired. When I asked if there was anything I could do to help, Professor Nazareth asked me to be his research assistant. And so it was that I was able to sit in on the Elvis course not only a second but even a third time. What struck me about the experience was that he did not teach the course the same way each spring. No, he kept surprising me by drawing new or different connections, by playing new threads of songs. He would play different material as well as new material we had discovered. That period of time was particularly fruitful in terms of his work on uncovering the deep mutual respect between Elvis and Jackie Wilson, and I benefitted from seeing how his research changed how he taught those sessions. Elvis As Anthology was never the same course twice. This will not surprise teachers, of course, but it was eye-opening for me as an undergraduate. It stuck with me, too, as I taught the same courses for several years at different colleges. The spirit of the class—what's been rebranded nowadays as "outcomes"—could hold true while the means of carrying everything out could evolve. I learned that what we do and how we do it matter, and that we can see and interpret anything through in any number of ways.

***

Teaching the first college course on Elvis Presley's art brought attention from all directions. Keith Morrison, before cementing his career in television as *Dateline*'s most popular true crime reporter, did a story on Professor Nazareth for the *Today Show*. When I reached out to Morrison regarding this Festschrift, he wrote back, "I remember Peter Nazareth and his Elvis ideas very well; his was one of the more memorable stories I've ever had the good fortune to cover. I'd love to know more about what happened in later years." The present volume, crafted in

Peter's spirit, hopefully sketches that story. Funnily enough, Morrison's news story became part of the course. Nazareth would show it to the students of Elvis As Anthology, challenging us to analyze Morrison's techniques in profiling him and, by extension, Presley.

Which is to say, Nazareth's Elvis ideas are really ideas about living—and not just living, but doing so cleverly, with a twinkle in the eye. On the face of it, the Elvis course was a deep dive on one particular artist, on the ways he articulated and twinned himself in voice, lyric, and performance. Students developed a foundational respect and understanding of an astonishing human being's work, all that went into it, and much of what spun off from it. For many of us in college in the '90s and 2000s, Elvis had died before we were born and yet his voice was still on the radio, his image ubiquitous in American and even world culture. He was undoubtedly one of the most influential artists of all time. And so getting to know his work was getting to know ourselves and our history.

All of that is significant in its own right, but here's the thing. Elvis was also just the subject matter at hand, in that what Nazareth was really teaching us was a suite of analytical skills that can be applied to anything one might study. There was the research he encouraged and modeled, for instance, in tracking down recordings by any number of musicians and artists, giving one access to a number of primary and secondary texts to examine and consider. But even more profoundly, and phenomenologically, he was giving us opportunities to practice listening, to practice watching, to practice the making of connections both intellectually and at the level of embodiment. We would tap our toes to the music he played, and then link that to the elements in the music bringing it about.

"What did you hear?" he would ask us after playing a string

of three versions of three recordings of the same song. Since no two of us heard the same way and brought different kinds of knowledge to the group, we were suddenly learning a lot from each other, too. This mode of learning sharpened students' abilities to both hear and see what is at play in a work of art—or a sequence of works of art—and, just as crucially, to speak to them. He challenged us to *read* material that others took for mere entertainment...or worse. For example, while some people write off Presley's films like *Girls! Girls! Girls!* (1962), *It Happened At The World's Fair* (1963), and *Paradise, Hawaiian Style* (1966), Nazareth would bring various musical numbers from them into an analysis of Elvis's role as a multicultural musician. Here Presley is singing and dancing with women and girls in traditional dress from cultures the world over, there he sings with a hundred musicians and dancers from various cultures of the Pacific Islands. Unpacking these elaborate productions together in class, the cynical (and lazy) reading of Elvis as an unsophisticated hillbilly quickly falls apart. What arises in its stead is, among other lively notions, an understanding that collaborative analysis expands appreciation. By considering an artist's work in all the ways we can think to, we discover there is a lot more to admire and learn from than we first thought.

Those techniques could be taught via any subject. So why Elvis? Nazareth has spoken about there being no prerequisite adoration or even like of Elvis's music for students. The course itself began after the untimely death of fellow professor, Jonathan Walton, who urged him to teach it. Nazareth had played for him and Lee Cloud Chuck Willis's "Feel So Bad" (1953) along with Elvis's version (1961), the three of them discussing the musical dialogue Elvis had opened with Willis. In this Nazareth heard "the colonial's loss of center, the center that has been taken away by colonialism, so the person knows he feels bad but does not know what to do about it" (Nazareth, "Elvis As Anthology" 45). Walton, astonished, remarked that nobody in America was listening, that he should teach an Elvis course to share these insights. One need not be a fan, and indeed fans would come to understand the music and movies in new ways. As he has explained, the course has been multi-modal from the beginning:

> I don't ask that my students should love Elvis before they come. I don't mind what they think, but that they should *listen*. And when I play the stuff—remember Jonathan's statement to people, 'They're not *listening*'—I play the original and then Elvis, [and] there's a complex dialogue that takes place. It's not just copying. It's reversing, turning upside down, Elvis sometimes removes words, sometimes changes words, sometimes combines many different people. So we go into history. We go into politics. We go into spirituality. And music. (qtd. in thelibrarychannel)

Nazareth's brilliance as an educator is that he hid a suite of survival skills in a course on an icon—someone larger than life—so that, instead of laying out all of the various means of analysis in a humdrum, bullet-pointed slideshow, he got students to pick them up, hands-on, while studying something undergrads love: popular music. My mother, who sat in on a class once, copped on to this immediately. A career teacher herself, she was grateful he had taken an interest in mentoring me. And all of his work to instill greater consciousness carries over into his other courses, too; I know because I took every course he taught. But when it came to Elvis As Anthology, and the students it drew spring to spring, there was something truly alchemical at work.

***

For Nazareth, a postcolonial literary critic and artist, everything is at stake. He and his family lived through the coup in Uganda and the Asian Expulsion that dispersed the already historically diasporic Goan community. They knew people who, in that time, vanished. He knew how dangerous the world can be long before I did, and more personally than I (pampered with privilege) do now at forty, and he has consistently throughout his career imparted to others means and ways that can help us get through hard passages. Students in his courses have encountered these firsthand—what he calls *trickster tactics*—but his interviews with authors, his fiction, and his scholarly work carry them, too. Take this from his monograph *In the Trickster Tradition* (1994), a study on three authors he argues to be tricksters: "[Andrew] Salkey, [Francis] Ebejer and [Ishmael] Reed seek to make us open doors which swing two ways, into the outer world and into ourselves: thus getting us to come to terms with our complex selves so that we can deal with and master a complex and dangerous world" (232-233). This focus acknowledges just how great the challenge of living is to each of us, individually and collectively at the same time. He often presents lessons he learned along the way in humorous ways. Take, for instance, the highlight of his fellowship at Yale University: A panel symposium of the editorial board of *MAD Magazine.* Or even one of his favorite tricksters of all, whose methods he studied all his life and has employed in surprising moments: Daffy Duck. Of course, anyone who has spent some time looking into popular satire, or the sophistication of those animated shorts produced throughout the middle decades of the twentieth century, will know Nazareth's definitely on to something. Close attention to those ways of maneuvering through the world had seen him through difficult times.

Kenya's greatest literary artist and critical theorist, Ngũgĩ wa Thiong'o, became friends with Nazareth at Makerere University College when they were undergraduates. Nazareth, Ngũgĩ recalls, was "the All-Makerere personality, a presence in music, sports, theater, student politics, and writing" (2). Both of them went on to complete postgraduate degrees at Leeds University, too. The time in England was not easy, Nazareth experiencing unabashed racism from the very instructors who were teaching him. Luckily, he married Mary Fernandes, a Goan woman from Tanzania, shortly after beginning his studies. They started their family while living in England. And there was the solid support of friends like Ngũgĩ.

Following the postgraduate degree, the young family moved back to Entebbe, where Peter had grown up. Many of the Goans living there worked in the Civil Service; that is what had drawn his father to move there from Goa. Peter's mother, also Goan, was born and raised in Malaysia. And so, Peter and his siblings were first-generation Ugandans. Peter, being the eldest, was returning to a large family and community that knew him well. He wanted to get into teaching at Makerere but the Civil Service was ready to employ him. They posted him to the Ministry of Finance and there he worked for many years, Peter and Mary soon welcoming a second daughter. Sometimes people are surprised to find out about this period in his professional life. A writer and literary critic working in governmental finances? And not only that, but also holding the job through a military coup. It astonishes. But Nazareth remembers much of that time in positive ways. His writing took off, both critically and creatively. "I was reeducating myself," he says, "because when I was in England I felt I had been miseducated under the colonial system" (qtd. in thelibrarychannel). In this period, as shown in the work he was doing in his free time as a literary critic, Nazareth was asking pertinent questions about the role of literature in East Africa and shining light on the novels and plays being written there. His critical attention appraised works by writers unknown to most scholars throughout the anglophone world. Most significantly, Nazareth's work also helped establish the paradigm of postcolonial theory that today is taught practically everywhere. In *Globalectics*, Ngũgĩ ranks Nazareth as a luminary alongside Gayatri Spivak, Edward Said, Homi Bhabha, Simon Gikandi, Abiola Irele, Anthony Appiah, Ali Mazrui, and Wole Soyinka (12, 53).

In August 1972, Idi Amin expelled all Asians carrying British passports. He went on to revise this: All Asians had to leave the country. Two weeks prior, Nazareth had published his first novel, *In a Brown Mantle*, which prophesied Goans having to leave Damibia, a fictitious African country, because they were not welcome anymore. In reality, it was happening. Despite the mass confusion, Nazareth kept working in the Ministry of Finance after this. Friends abroad—known and unknown—worked to grant him the Seymour Lustman Fellowship to Yale University so he and his wife and daughters had a place to land at the beginning of 1973; much of the rest of his family were welcomed by Canada, which had responded to the humanitarian crisis. At Yale, along with the *MAD Magazine* editors and Alice Walker, he also met Charles T. Davis, the preeminent African American scholar at the time, who told him the University of Iowa was the place for him. Davis made sure Nazareth was invited by Paul Engle, Hualing Nieh, and Darwin T. Turner to be an Honorary Fellow in the International Writing Program (IWP) later that year.

In *Community of Imagination*, Gerald Krell's 1973 documentary about the IWP, we can find Nazareth, who had just arrived in Iowa, succinctly summarizing some of the challenges of being a postcolonial writer at that moment:

> The writer from the third world begins to realize that he's facing all kinds of questions, like who is he writing for? Who's going to read him? Why is he writing? And then he realizes that actually he comes from a situation where he has been led to believe that all writing, all culture, comes from outside. It all comes from Europe. And so he then says, "Well, I've got to counteract that. So that means I have to write specifically for my people." Then he has to define, "Who are my people?" Now: "Why do I write?" One of the reasons why I write is to remove this great burden of foreign culture. (qtd. in University of Iowa)

This line of thought, expressed with urgency, speaks to the way his world had been turned upside down. As Ngũgĩ has noted, "His Makerere stories and plays had exuded love for the Uganda he grew up in" (224). The loss was a collective trauma for the Ugandan Goans and Asians. It was also, as these horrid events always are, an individual trauma. Who is a writer exiled from Uganda, where he was born, who now lives in the American heartland? If that question was not yet setting in, surely it would before long.

But Nazareth was not alone. His family had come with him and there can be no doubt that they have always been key in his ability to thrive. Tamil writer Ashokamitran, recalling his experiences in the IWP, bears witness to the homesickness of the Nazareths' particular exile:

> Mary, Peter and their children lived in Iowa City now.

> They had never talked of their plight—of having had to change home and country suddenly, repeatedly, due to events of contemporary history—to anyone. Peter alone had remarked once, 'You have a home to go back to, and a country. What's there for me?' He always spoke about Uganda, wrote about Uganda. Uganda had entirely inhabited him; Uganda, which he could never again claim as his own. (149)

In Ashokamitran's memoir, he shares that on his final day in Iowa City, he had not packed his bags and it was Mary Nazareth who got him and his belongings ready for the journey home. As he put it, "Mary knew what had to be done" (150). Indeed, when I met Mary, I suddenly understood why, having gone through such turmoil, Peter had exceled. She is remarkable, his match in every way. She is both kindness and action, someone who is never fooled for a second—and she forges friendships for life. And while Peter transitioned to lecturing in the Afro-American Studies Program and teaching on the tenure track, Mary made her own long and invaluable career working in the IWP. Her reputation stands as tall as his does to writers around the globe. Past participants in the program rightly speak of them as a duo, a team of two. As Peter once put it himself, "my achievements, mysterious as they might sometimes seem, are in great measure Mary's as well" (*Third World Writer* xix). Their daughters, Kathy and Monique, and their families have also given them even more to be proud of.

Remember that Nazareth had initially wanted to go into teaching when he graduated from Leeds University, but the Civil Service beckoned. After years of working as a bureaucrat, now, at the University of Iowa, he had the chance to become the professor he had long wanted to be, all while advising in the

IWP. In 1977, he became Assistant Professor of English and Afro-American Studies. Three years later, he was tenured as an Associate Professor. And in 1985 he became a Professor of English and African American World Studies. He also chaired African American World Studies and the African Studies Program. Throughout this phase of his working life, his creative work included literary criticism, short stories, and a second novel. He also published an array of scholarly work on African literature, Caribbean literature, Ishmael Reed, Joseph Conrad, Singapore literature, and Goan literature. Cruise through decades of *World Literature Today* and you will find more than 160 book reviews he wrote, a temporal trail of literary breadcrumbs attesting to a reading taste as broad and far-reaching as it gets.

Add to this the fiction. His second novel, *The General Is Up*, takes readers back to the fictitious African country, Damibia, which was the setting of *In a Brown Mantle*. Nazareth has always been explicit in conversation that Damibia is not Uganda, not merely a cipher, and the dictator looming over the second novel is not a thinly veiled depiction of Amin. But I can also hear Peter reminding me what D. H. Lawrence said in "The Spirit of Place"—to never trust the teller, trust the tale. By that metric, *The General Is Up* affirms the trauma of the Asian Expulsion of 1972, bears witness to it in imaginative ways, just as Kurt Vonnegut's *Slaughterhouse-Five* brought the Allied bombing of Dresden in World War II to light for the victims, the survivors, and the people just finding out it even happened. Nazareth's fantasy of Damibia, dreamed in Uganda and Iowa and first published in India and then Canada, speaks to those powers W. H. Auden believed we are lived by and only pretend to understand.

Quite simply, Nazareth's abilities in balancing criticism and artistry with family and pedagogy set the bar high.

Incidentally, he has been recognized in many ways. Writers he studied paid attention to him; Reed, for instance, named him in his novel *Japanese By Spring* for pointing out his use of some colonial language: "Perhaps it was Peter Nazareth's catching Ishmael Reed red-handed anglicizing Yoruba (Yoruban)" (122). As far as tributes go, being invoked (positively, even!) in a novel by your subject is certainly a feather in the cap. And when it comes to his experiences in teaching, Nazareth also taught correspondence courses through the Center for Credit Programs, being awarded the Distinguished Independent Study Course from the National University Continuing Education Association.

***

I mentioned that I took all of Professor Nazareth's courses. Heeding his guidance, I grew a lot. I had always leaned toward storytelling but found myself becoming an academic writer under his tutelage. And the Elvis class's rubric was no walk in the park. Students had options of writing two fifteen-page papers or one sustained essay of thirty pages. That is daunting for an undergraduate student, but I went for the latter, as did many other students over the years. My essay, the longest I had written up to that point, was on comedian Andy Kaufman's lifelong obsession with Elvis and the way he impersonated him in his acts. Kaufman had also written a one-man play called *God*, which is about an allegorical Elvis meeting the Creator. Engaging with these materials in an academic context really stretched what I could do at the time, finishing out my sophomore year.

After that, I took an independent study course with Nazareth over a summer where I read all of Ngũgĩ wa Thiong'o's novels and wrote essays on them. The final project was the most difficult, with Nazareth challenging me to write on Ngũgĩ and

Elvis. As far as I could see at the outset, it was an impossibility, the artists occupying utterly different realms. All too easily, it could just become a weak comparison/contrast essay. He suggested finding places of intersection between them. Sitting with that, I did start noticing places where each one was making intriguing, insightful comments on the same subject: the Devil! Ngũgĩ's *Devil on the Cross* was (and remains) my favorite of his novels; meanwhile, Elvis left a trail of takes on the Devil in nine songs throughout his catalog. I also plunged into literary criticism, finding Gĩtahi Gĩtĩtĩ and David Hulm, whose articles contextualized Ngũgĩ's work and even drew lines between Ngũgĩ and Bob Marley. I found both artists depicting the Devil in nuanced ways, as well as in the languages particular to their personal cultural histories. In terms of completing that final essay, the Devil turned out to be a winner. As Nazareth closes his short story "Eccentric Ferns," "Sometimes the Devil cannot be beaten" (132). It remains the most difficult essay I have ever written, but it also broke my notions of what scholarship had to be. One could truly find plenty to unpack where, to begin with, it looked like there wasn't even a chest to hold treasure. Fruitful work could come from an endeavor initially assumed to be inconceivable.

These projects, encouraged and assessed by Nazareth, led directly to my honors thesis: *Lennon in the Key of Elvis.* My years-long obsession with John Lennon's music transformed into the capstone of my undergraduate education. I was prepared for it thanks to Professor Nazareth. I remember one of the students in our cohort, a genuinely collegiate fellow and so insightful on dense critical theory—he would rattle off Derrida or Adorno like poetry—shocked us all when he failed to turn in a thesis. It turned out he had not written anything all along. Standing at the end of that process with the work I had done made me so much more grateful for Nazareth's help and presence. He supported me. He saw me through. He did not hold my hand because he had faith in me, and he counseled me on inevitable issues where I needed clarification. How truly fortunate I was.

After I graduated from the University of Iowa, I spent a year in England earning a master's degree in Creative Writing at Lancaster University, not terribly far from Leeds where he had earned his. When I returned to Iowa, I visited him and Mary to catch up. He congratulated me on the achievement and then said, with great assurance, "Now your re-education begins." I made to ask what he meant by that, but he was already telling me. "All the things you've learned now need to be unlearned as you move through the world. And you will unlearn them."

This was something I grew up hearing in my favorite movie. Yoda says practically the same thing to Luke Skywalker in *The Empire Strikes Back*: "You must unlearn what you have learned." But it is also an echo from Nazareth's own history. Recall his perspective on his time working in the Civil Service after leaving Leeds: "I was reeducating myself, because when I was in England I felt I had been miseducated under the colonial system" (qtd. in thelibrarychannel). In many ways, this psychological focus he gave me has kept me questioning not just my education but education itself. This is for the better. It is both easy and limiting to take what we have learned at face value. There remain questions, should we choose to ask them, about why we were educated the way we were. Where was I miseducated in the American system? Perhaps there is no destination to such an inquiry; "arriving" could be as dangerous as accepting one's education as it happened. Here was my finest professor instructing me yet again, teaching me the positivity of reexamination, of looking for blind spots—both my own and those of the system that conditioned me—and adapting to the dynamics of life as it unfolds.

Some years later, when I went to Ireland—a postcolonial nation—to further my education, I found myself turning back to Nazareth's guidance. I was studying Literature of the Americas at Trinity College Dublin on a taught master's program, blessed with two supportive professors, Philip Coleman and Melanie Otto. When our cohort pitched our individual dissertation topics, I was so relieved when they accepted mine. I wanted to historicize the song lyrics of Jesse 'Ed' Davis, a Kiowa rock guitarist who in the 1970s put out three LPs that express his autobiographical experiences in the US. This work was immensely rewarding, as Davis had never truly been given his due. The way I knew his music was through Elvis As Anthology, where Nazareth played his and John Trudell's brilliant song about Elvis, "Baby Boom Che." Bob Dylan had called Davis and Trudell's collaboration "the album of the year" in 1986, yet Davis, who died in 1988, remained largely unknown. Nazareth had planted the seed there in his class that I circled back to and had the chance to nurture and tend. The result was joyous scholarship that expanded my abilities, earned my second master's, and eventually saw publication in *American Indian Quarterly*. These successes, which shined light on an artist we should have been appreciating more for decades, all grew out of Nazareth's mentorship. Later, when I was offered a book contract for my PhD research, I signed it at Peter and Mary's dining room table. When that book was published, I dedicated it to him. You see, my accomplishments point back to his instruction, his kindness, and his presence. I would not have done much of the work I've done if not for him.

***

The contributions to this Festschrift are offered by colleagues, friends, and former students. Our idea in this collective effort was to share our work in the spirit of Peter's scholarship, artistry, and life. As he put it himself, "I always wanted to write everything" ("Twenty-First-Century Foreword" xlii). As such, consider this Festschrift to be a steaming pot of gumbo ya-ya.[1] Here we have an international medley of thoughtfully sourced and shared ingredients: articles on literature, essays on music, a short story, an interview, and poetry expressing what cannot be expressed any other way. Peter has shown us all along that the literary critic and the literary artist need not be separate people—they can be one person doing it all, exploring life intellectually and artistically without sacrificing one for the other. This is because, as he points out, art and criticism entwine with engagement that can urge us to do and be better:

> Writing of a country or a nation needs empathetic literary criticism. There is a creative relationship between writer and critic. Fiction, poetry and drama are frequently deeper than the writer realizes because things come through the work which the writer does not realize but the critics can discover. Writers can learn about their works from critics. But as I said earlier, quoting D. H. Lawrence, critics need to be educated in the deepest and widest sense of the word. ("Twenty-First-Century Foreword" xliii)

He has set the finest example for those of us who refuse to limit ourselves to one aspect of our potential. His works—especially that which he has done in teaching—prove that the best we can

[1] Peter taught us that *gumbo ya-ya* can refer to gumbo so tasty it makes people cry, "Ya-ya!" or, in Cajun, a situation where everybody speaks at the same time. It was also considered as a possible title for what became Elvis's 1962 movie *Girls! Girls! Girls!*

do is bring forth whatever it is only we can bring forth. We reckon there is a play within us? We can write that play. We notice a pattern occurring in dynamic ways across a spread of novels? We can research and write an article, even a monograph on it. We have an urge to paint the protagonist of a novel that has been working on us in mysterious ways? We can paint the character's portrait—which, incidentally, his student Michelle Van Ness did in his African Literature course. Her painting, which has hung on the wall in Nazareth's office for decades, is of Maru, the titular character of Bessie Head's 1971 novel. When she asked if she could do this painting as part of her final project, a nontraditional appendix to the paper, he said yes. Over time, he came to see that she had cleverly used him as the model for Maru; indeed, the figure sits in the chair so much like Peter would on my visits to his office. For these reasons, and others left open to analytical interpretation, Van Ness's art adorns the cover of this collection.

Here is to Professor Nazareth as he crosses the threshold to Professor Emeritus. What is retirement if not a fresh opportunity to apply those honed trickster tactics? Thank you, Peter, for all you have done for so many.

S. G. Ellerhoff
Eugene, Oregon
2021

## WORKS CITED

Ashokamitran. *Mole!* Translated by N. Kalyan Raman, Orient BlackSwan, 2010.

Morrison, Keith. "Now that was a surprise!" *Twitter* direct message, received by S. G. Ellerhoff, 17 Jan. 2020.

Nazareth, Peter. "Eccentric Ferns." *Short Story International*, vol. 4, no.

19, April 1980, pp. 127-132.

———. "Elvis as Anthology." *In Search of Elvis*, edited by Vernon Chadwick, Westview Press, 1997, pp. 37-72.

———. *In the Trickster Tradition: The Novels of Andrew Salkey, Francis Ebejer and Ishmael Reed*. Bogle-L'Ouverture Press, 1994.

———. *The Third World Writer: His Social Responsibility*. Kenya Literature Bureau, 1978.

———. "Twenty-First-Century Foreword." *Pivoting on the Point of Return: Modern Goan Literature*, edited by Peter Nazareth. Goa 1556 and Broadway Book Centre, 2010.

Ngũgĩ wa Thiong'o. *Birth of a Dream Weaver: A Writer's Awakening*. New Press, 2016.

———. *Globalectics*. Columbia University Press, 2012.

Reed, Ishmael. *Japanese By Spring*. Penguin, 1993.

Sheff, David. *The Playboy Interviews: John Lennon & Yoko Ono*. Playboy Press, 1981.

thelibrarychannel. "One of a Kind: Peter Nazareth." *YouTube*, 19 Jun. 2017, https://youtu.be/ZqI9TmOsFgs.

University of Iowa. "Community of the Imagination (1973) dir. Gerald Krell." *YouTube*, 24 Sep. 2010, https://youtu.be/DlPgdxU6o0M.

# CHRONOLOGY

1940 – Born in Uganda, then a colony of the United Kingdom.

1962 – BA (Hons) in English from Makerere University College in Kampala, Uganda.

1964 – Marries Mary Fernandes, from Tanzania.

1965 – Postgraduate diploma in English Studies from Leeds University, UK.
Returns to Uganda, working his way up in the Civil Service to become a Senior Finance Officer in the Ministry of Finance.

1971 – Idi Amin becomes President of Uganda through a coup.

1972 – *Literature and Society in Modern Africa*, published by East African Literature Bureau (EALB).
First novel, *In a Brown Mantle*, published by EALB.
August – Amin expels all Asians, including Ugandans of Asian descent. Nazareth is rendered stateless, but issued a British passport.

1973 – January – Awarded the Seymour Lustman Fellowship at Yale University, allowing him, his wife, and daughters safe passage to the United States. Much of the rest of his family are welcomed by Canada and England (though they later emigrate to Canada, too).
August – Made an Honorary Fellow in the International Writing Program (IWP) at the University

of Iowa. Peter and Mary have lived in Iowa City and Coralville since this time.

1974 – *An African View of Literature*, published by Northwestern University Press.

1976 – *Two Radio Plays*, originally produced for the BBC African Service, published by EALB.

1977 – Becomes Assistant Professor of English and African American World Studies at the University of Iowa.

1978 – *The Third World Writer: His Social Responsibility*, published by Kenya Literature Bureau.

1980 – Becomes Associate Professor of English and African American World Studies.

1981 – *African Writing Today*, edited for *Pacific Moana Quarterly*.

1984 – Second novel, *The General Is Up*, first published by Writers Workshop (published again in 1991 by TSAR Books, reprinted in 1998, and revised and republished in 2013 by Goa 1556).
Serves as Vice President of African Literature Association (1984-1985).

1985 – Becomes Professor of English and African American World Studies.
Serves President of African Literature Association (1985-1986).

1991-1992 – Chair of African American World Studies.

1992 – First teaches Elvis As Anthology, which captures worldwide media attention.

1992-1994 – Chair of African Studies Program.

1994 – *In The Trickster Tradition: The Novels of Andrew Salkey, Francis Ebejer and Ishmael Reed*, published by Bogle-L'Ouverture Press.
Awarded the Distinguished Independent Study Course from the National University Continuing Education Association.

1995 – Attends first International Conference on Elvis Presley at the University of Mississippi in Oxford, organized by Vernon Chadwick.

1997 – "Elvis As Anthology" essay published in *In Search of Elvis*, edited by Vernon Chadwick and published by Westview Press.

2000 – *Critical Essays on Ngũgĩ wa Thiong'o*, edited volume for Twayne Publishers.

2002 – *Uganda South Asians Exodus: Kololian Perspectives*, edited volume for University of Toronto Press.

2008 – *Edwin Thumboo: Creating a Nation Through Poetry*, published by Ethos Books.

2009 – Donates "The Peter Nazareth Collection," comprising

thirty years of recorded interviews with international writers, to the University of Iowa Libraries. These interviews have been digitized and are available online.

2010 – *Pivoting on the Point of Return: Modern Goan Literature*, edited for Goa 1556 and Broadway Book Centre.

2013 – *Elvis: Rewriting the World Through Multicultural Movies*, published by Goa 1556.

2014 – *Re-Membering Singapore*, published by Goa 1556.

2021 – Retires from teaching at the University of Iowa, having taught through the COVID-19 pandemic in his final year of instruction.

# THE PLACE OF MY BIRTH

*For Peter Nazareth*

I rotate in spaces where
Questions are taboo.
I have grown up not knowing
Why dislocation
Sits like a yawning lion
On the green hills that
Lent me life.

I hover behind trees
Unable to piece together
The divided hills of our history.
The houses in Old Kampala
Struggle to show their faces despite
The canopy of algae.
They remind me of milk gone sour.
They stand there distortions
Of their original selves.
Those houses cannot tell me their story
I pass them longingly figuring out
Forms and voices
But they are silent.

In this land where silence sits
Like a priest at a raised altar
My mind hungers for the Indian story
I want to wrestle it out
Of the clamped jaws of History
I need to hear

What volcanoes erupted here
While I still slept in the
Womb of my mother.
I want to touch and reconcile the
Violence vomited on the
Place where
My umbilical cord is buried.
I choose to know
So the trapped heat
In my head makes
Meaning to my heart.

I want to reconcile me
With the place of my early footprints
I want liberty to cry over the
Wounds in my brain.
I thirst to know of the little girls
Who sat on the benches
That are shielded by the palms
On the banks of the Nile.
The little girls denied
The pleasure of home
And the strange laughter
Of thunderstorms.
I long to touch the tears that were denied a drying.
The crying children that hover in the distances
Created by flying history
Have become loud voices
In my head.

Susan Nalugwa Kiguli

# THE MOST SACRED EGO

Each morning when I rise
Why, my Lord, I ask
Hath this unsaluted *onus*
On me compelled
Which in a single swipe
Effaces
Whatever distinctions
*Altos* or *falsettos*
Elsewhere encored
As hither
Cowed and crouched
I sit
In a *chambre*
Intentionally made
For one
Whereunto swiping
In a self-attuned *timbre*
My most sacred ego
A task
I wouldn't dare entrust
Another
*Albeit* a task
Another wouldn't conduct
For money's sake
Or honor's take
Not e'en the scavenger

Elsewhere despised
Seemingly this moment alas
Besides me crouched
And grinning
And bragging
And betting
And swiping quite well
indeed
His indubious own!

But when I see poverty
And injustice
Harrowing some
While others thrive
In wealth
Power
And sophistry
I pause and think
Of the queer God
Who created man:
*Dictum … Factum … Rectum*
What omni*bum!*
*Ah!*
The Lord knew mighty well
His job
Mankind saving
In that desperately last
Discreet *erratum*
Once, an unpleasant task
But nigh alas
A pleasurable revelation
As I bow and swipe and *glow*
And in bowing behold
Kings, Popes, Aristocrats
Communists
E'en *dictators!*
Each surreptitiously bent
And swiping deftly well
His unenvied own
In an unbroken cycle
Of innate *concertos*
To the undated scavenger
Who mankind taught
In inauctionable onus
First thing each morning
Past bolting to ye temple
Defaulted for one
Whereunto reconciling
In solemn consternation
The cumbrous disparity
Betwixt hope and despair
Want and excess
Asset and liability
And thereupon remain
Acoustically blessed
And indemnified
Until the next cantorical *alto*
Or lurking *falsetto!*

Dom Martin

# Interview Given by Professor Peter Nazareth to Okoiti Omtatah

Austin Bukenya

In 1993, Professor Peter Nazareth [PN] kindly answered a few questions regarding his novel *The General Is Up*, put to him by Mr. Okoiti Omtatah [OO] of Nairobi on my behalf for my PhD research. This interview is referred to a number of times in the body of my study and was included as Appendix B to the final dissertation, *An Idiom of Blood: Pragmatic Readings of the Ugandan Novel.* An article was published from this work in *Uganda Journal* (vol. 46, December 2000, pp. 17-37). The following edited extracts from the interview not only provide useful insights into *The General Is Up* and its genesis but also reveal Professor Nazareth's wide-ranging concerns about Ugandan literature and public affairs. An audiocassette tape of the interview has been deposited in the archives of the Literature Department, Makerere University, Kampala.

PN: This is Peter Nazareth. I am being interviewed in Coralville, Iowa, on 17th October 1993 by Okoiti Omtatah on behalf of Austin Bukenya. The very first question Okoiti has asked me is: "What motivated you to write *The General Is Up*?"

I began by saying that I began writing what became *The General Is Up* while I was in Uganda. This was after I had written and published my first novel, *In a Brown Mantle. In a Brown Mantle* was published and was launched with full publicity in Uganda, when the things that it had prophesied actually came true.

The coup took place while the novel was with the publishers, and the expulsion of the Asians was announced nine days after the novel was launched in Kampala. With expulsion, I abandoned the fragments that I was writing, and I got a fellowship to Yale for the first novel, and that's how I left Uganda in early 1973.

Then I came to the International Writing Program—that was in 1973. There was first in my program that year a writer named José Antonio Bravo, who told me that all the stories I was telling him of Uganda and Idi Amin—he was having nightmares and he wanted to write a novel, but it was *my* novel and I should write it. … And I didn't actually do it, but the following year there was [Cyprian] Ekwensi, who said something very similar. … Ekwensi said, "By God! The novel is in your head; go and write it." … And then Ekwensi said to me, "What do you feel like now that you've written it?" And I said, "I feel very relieved, as though I'm recovering from a long illness."

So that's what it was. It was a novel that I was obsessed with and *just had to tell* because of the really terrible things that had happened in the country.

I should slightly qualify this by saying that I had, before getting to write the whole novel, I had sent that one chapter that I wrote in Uganda to Uganda at the request of Ejiet Komolo, who was editing *Dhana*, and he published it, under the title "The Institute." He wrote to me and said that he found it quite remarkable and he hoped I would finish the novel.

OO: Are some of the incidents in your novel based on real-life happenings?

PN: Yes, the novels *are* based on many real-life incidents. I remember, though, Achebe saying that when he wrote, *he* had to tone things down from real life because they were so unbelievable. ... But you *will* also note that there are some differences from real life. For example, the term is not used, "Asians," it's "East Indians," and ... the period [of the expulsion] is not three months but it's "by the next moon." ... But, broadly speaking, yes, there are incidents which are taken from real life, though the language is mine.

OO: Which, to you, are the most memorable sequences in your novel, and why?

PN: You know, now I will have to speak not so much as the person who wrote the novel as the person who reads it. There are some scenes that I like very much, like: I like very much the scene of the expulsion at the airport. This is Chapter 24. In fact, it was the first, once the novel was completed, this was the first item that got published. Achebe published it in *Okike* and that was a real spur, again, to me. At that time I used the title "Departure," and that chapter, which could almost be read as a journalistic account of the scene at the airport was published in many different places. It was published in Toronto and, in translation, it was published in Polish, in Hebrew, in Japanese. So that is one of my great favourite ... chapters. And that's a chapter that actually grounds the whole novel and gives it seriousness.

There's a lot of other things in the novel that are very funny, and I enjoy them very much. I particularly enjoy reading the last chapter, before the Epilogue, because it works very well and is very funny. I read it last year [1992] at the end of the Andrew Salkey conference, at the Commonwealth Institute, and the audience really laughed at the section when the bullet strikes the head of the General and bounces off and strikes the photo of the Queen of England hanging on a wall.

There are other chapters in the novel that are very funny. ... One section I don't like very much when I read it is the one where the character David D'Costa has all these citizenship problems, because that's so close to my own experience I don't like to read it.

OO: Your novel describes several patently violent incidents. What was your purpose in portraying these incidents?

PN: You know, a lot of the time the violence in the novel is very indirect. There is a real parallel here with Ekwensi's *Survive the Peace*, which he wrote, you know, he was writing his and I was writing mine. Much of the violence is indirect: that is, somebody talks about it or someone mentions; you hardly ever see the violence directly in front of your own eyes. I mean, even that scene of the bullets striking the General is kind of stylized like a comic book. The only real incident of violence you see before your eyes is when an ordinary person, that is, one of the common people, is roughed up by the soldiers at the airport.

Now, a lot of the incidents of violence are of course based

on things that happened in real life, which created the whole tone of violence through that time, that period and the society. But you know … this novel *is* stylized, and in the early incident of Captain Oma, the question is: Why is this Captain Oma, who is haunting the General, the same Captain Oma whom the General has killed? Who is this Captain Oma? And at the end of the novel—I mean, the last chapter, that is—the same Captain Oma seems to suddenly turn up and grow larger and larger, and come and grab the General up and lift him to his feet, and the General is shooting at him—but nobody else sees Captain Oma, only the General. So, there is a scene in the novel, when the cook is calling out to *Mungu*, to God, and you have to ask yourself: is it that, at the very end of this novel, in the Epilogue, does it turn out that one of the characters who was in the novel actually ran away but wrote a novel, and in this novel he punished people who deserved to be punished in real life but were not punished? In other words, could this Captain Oma be a way in which the person who wrote the novel gave the General a conscience to haunt him out of what the General himself did?

OO: What responses have you received to your novel? Which of these do you regard as significant, and why?

PN: I have received a lot of responses to this novel; the curious thing is that this novel became famous even before it was published, that is, before it was published as a whole, because many chapters were published in many different places. I've mentioned some already but chapters were published in a journal called *New Quest* in Bombay, in *Pacific Moana Quarterly* in New Zealand, and so on. And, when you publish chapters by themselves, they have a different kind of meaning—I mean, they imply a whole novel which may or may not be this novel from which they come. So, I have had many responses. Most of the responses are to those so-called—well, I shouldn't say "so-called"—but the chapters are so serious that they seem to be a nonfiction account of what happened. When I read the novel aloud, or when I teach the novel, then there are people who realize that there are scenes in the novel that are very funny, that you actually laugh at, true—true: this is the kind of humour where you laugh to keep from crying, and I think of it as a very Ugandan kind of humour, because in Uganda people do laugh at serious things, but there is a special way of laughing at serious things.

OO: Did you have a specific kind of readership in mind? And if so, how would you describe this readership?

PN: Well, that is a pretty difficult question… But I could say yes, I did. You know, when I started writing my fiction in Uganda, that is when I wrote my first novel and the short stories, I was thinking of the Ugandan audience and more generally the East African audience. … My idea was to write in a language that was readable and got across to anybody who could read. Of course, the limitation is that it's in English. But it would be a way of writing that would be easy to follow, and particularly … it would be oral. You would hear the sound, so that the thing can be read aloud. And so, that's the audience that I'm thinking of primarily. … I felt that Uganda had to learn its own history and politics—it has to learn about itself from itself.

OO: Mr. Nazareth, if I may put in a question of my own … what message did you intend your novel to have for the Indians who were deported from Uganda?

PN: You know, sometimes a writer can reflect what people feel and think. … The novel will show the connectedness of all the different peoples of East Africa and will show, furthermore, that a great deal of the problems arose out of colonialism and neo-colonialism, although *we* contributed to it with our lack of understanding and perhaps sometimes even selfish motivations. But the one advantage that I could have dealing with Asians generally and Goans particularly in the novel is to bring a wider dimension of colonialism into the picture, because Goans had a long experience of Portuguese colonial rule, and then there was the Indian colonial rule under the British—I mean, the rule in India of the British. … The thing was to give a whole story of everybody there, but present it in a way which could give people power. I mean, when you read this novel, you feel you have some power over the events. You know, it's a funny novel, and humour is life-affirming…

OO: Did you deliberately adopt some specific literary, stylistic or structural devices in your novel? … What were your reasons, if any, for adopting these devices?

PN: You know, those early pages… I was not conscious of it at all, although in Uganda people did say such things. Somebody would say something very striking. Like a nun said to me, "The General is afraid of God because he can't throw God into the lake." … But, as for Chapter 26, the reason why it is short and just a few lines, and the rest of the page is blank, is that, after something so short happens, you have this whole blank, where … your emotions fill in the blank. You know, where you see how badly the servants are treated here. I mean, the officials come and just kick them out. They are told to leave within a day, with all their belongings, or else the police would be informed to come and throw them out. And then you have the blank space, and you can think: what about these servants? And in fact, the very next chapter [Chapter 27], you will notice that that is the chapter which is narrated by the cook, that is the cook who was working for David D'Costa. … The cook is left alone and the cook is talking about his experiences working for the Costas, and he has his own judgement of them, he has his own judgement of which Goans were good and which were not good, and what the life is like as a cook, and what are all the good things and the bad things and so on. But you know, when you get to the very end … then you have to think and say: "Wait a moment. Did the cook actually write this chapter? Does a person like the cook have a chance to tell his own story?" It is true that he has a certain perspective into the world, which we sometimes forget. We think that ordinary people, or servants, have no way of seeing the world. … But do they have a chance to talk and tell their story? Well, the suggestion is no. Therefore, the novel is suggesting, until such a time as they have the power to tell their own story, somebody who is sympathetic can tell the story in *their* words. But please bear in mind this is a transitional point. It is until such a time as they can speak for themselves. So, that is one of the stylistic devices, though, again I must tell you that, as far as I know, this is something I realised after I wrote it, and not before.

OO: You have probably read other books (both fiction and non-fiction) about the period of terror, violence and war in Uganda. Which are these and what is your assessment of them?

PN: Well, I've written a long chapter in the book edited by G. D. Killam [*The Writing of East and Central Africa*]. Even before that I wrote something shorter and published in *Rikka* in Canada. … My thesis is that the rise to power of a figure like Idi Amin is anticipated in Ugandan literature, as a consequence … of decolonisation and neocolonialism. Then, a lot of literature is dealing with his terrible presence on the scene. And some anticipates his departure, with fears that he will come back. … Idi Amin was a very complex figure… He was extremely good at using the international media, probably the best at using the media of all the leaders in the world… So, I myself approached the whole period from many different angles. There is this novel, there is a short piece of fiction I wrote shortly after this, which is published under the title "Rosie's Theme." Then I have written nonfiction about that time … and then some literary criticism. …

I think that clearly Idi Amin looms so large in Uganda that his presence and his consequences have to be dealt with for a long time by Ugandans. … So, I think that many, many, many novels written by Ugandans about Amin by Ugandans—and it is very important to look at novels by Ugandans (and sometimes Ugandans use pseudonyms)—very important to look at them and get a complex picture. Because what can happen if we don't do this is—and it's already happened by the way—is that outsiders, who have

> no interest in Uganda, real interest, or who seek to continue exploiting Uganda … dismiss the whole experience in terms of stereotypes. Ugandans have to take over control of their own stories…

# AMIN IS DEAD

*For Peter Nazareth*

Like Buffaloes charging against the sun
Sweeping up dust to litter the sky
The news arrived
Via a friend then another and another.

Amin is dead.

What do you do with such news?
Then a joke came
From one friend and then another and another
A symbolic image of the man
Blood and laughter.

But what do you do with such news?
How do you weave into melody
woes carried so long?
How do you put to rest
Grief that has never hoped
And will never.

How are we expected
To bear this news
To empty compounds
With graves half dug
To homes that closed
Three decades ago?
Where in the shades that replaced voices
Are we supposed to tell this news?

How do you expect us
To call our neighbours
Knowing we no longer have any
And give them mats
So we can exhume our
Grief and nurse it to sleep
So we can wonder at the irony
That had a body
Children and wives
Who are sad now like we were long before
And will continue to ache forever.
A nation in exile.

Life is lost in mirrors these days
Three heads are standing on one neck
My mind floats
Between reality and disbelief.

Susan Nalugwa Kiguli

# THE LAST KING OF AFRICA: THE REPRESENTATION OF IDI AMIN IN UGANDAN DICTATORSHIP NOVELS†

Oliver Lovesey

Idi Amin Dada (1925–2003), self-proclaimed President of Uganda (1971–79) after a military coup against Milton Obote, may be the prototype of the brutal African dictator. He was a masterful media manipulator who ruled through the power of both a bewitching charisma and spectacles of unimaginable terror. A man of questionable sanity, though supremely capable of manipulating such a reputation to his benefit, Amin claimed to be the last "uncrowned" King of Scotland, though in his surreal flamboyance he was rivaled by Jean-Bédel Bokassa, who had himself crowned as the emperor of the Central African Republic in a ceremony modeled on that of Napoleon.[1] Amin was a homicidal, kleptocratic megalomaniac who drained the national treasury, gutted his country's infrastructure, murdered nearly half a million Ugandans, threatened war with three of his neighbours, and directly or indirectly inaugurated genocidal actions that have contributed to the ongoing destabilization of much of central Africa. He may be seen as the precursor of the murderous and possibly insane Joseph Kony, whose Lord's Resistance Army continues to operate with its child soldiers in northern Uganda and elsewhere today. Though Kony was indicted in 2005 by the International Criminal Court on charges

† Originally published in *Unmasking the African Dictator: Essays on Postcolonial African Literature*, edited by Gĩchingiri Ndĩgĩrĩgĩ (2014). Reproduced here with permission from The University of Tennessee Press.

of crimes against humanity and war crimes, he remains at large.[2]

As the Arab Spring or Jasmine Revolution that has witnessed the demise of dictators and dictatorships throughout North Africa enters the fall and winter of its hope and challenge, it is difficult to appreciate the absolutism enjoyed by dictators such as Idi Amin over three decades ago. He fashioned himself as a pro-colonial stalwart and also as an anticolonial provocateur at will, playing the game of global, Cold War power politics for personal gain. Amin had been a member of a British colonial regiment, the King's African Rifles, and he had taken part in anti-Mau Mau (Kenya Land and Freedom Army) military actions in Kenya, as one of what Giles Foden calls the "colonial bloodhounds" (129).[3] He was widely admired for his athletic prowess in swimming, boxing, and rugby, but feared for his clandestine involvement in the affairs of Sudan and the Congo as well as illegal activities. Facing arrest for atrocities and smuggling, Amin staged a coup, stating that he would hold elections and free political prisoners. A week later the semi-literate Amin declared himself president and rapidly established Uganda as a military state and began a series of moves against all intellectuals as well as a virtual policy of ethnic cleansing.[4] Amin had styled himself a Field Marshal in the postcolonial Ugandan army, and in the mid-1970s he was the Chair of the Organization of African Unity. He had appeared to be the model of the procolonial postcolonial ruler until his outrages made him a liability to the former colonial overlords and he sought the fraternity of other dictators in Libya and East Germany.

Amin's police state would quickly become what Henry Kyemba, the health minister, would describe as "a state of blood."[5] In 1972, he expropriated property from Asians and Europeans in Uganda, and in August of that year expelled nearly 100,000 "people of East Indian origin, extraction, or ancestry"

(Nazareth 111), many Ugandan-born, leading to economic collapse. The 1976 Israeli hostage crisis at Entebbe airport and the Israeli military's daring rescue in Operation Entebbe intensified the growing international condemnation of the Amin regime, and the following year he claimed to be the Conqueror of the British Empire. His increasingly erratic behaviour in this period sparked widespread rumours that he was mentally ill and that he engaged in cannibalism.

Amin's self-mythologizing and catachrestic modes of expression gained much Western media attention, though he was represented as a comic buffoon and, in racist fashion, as a typical African dictator rather than an opportunistic fascist. Recent texts such as *Dictators' Homes: Lifestyles of the World's Most Colourful Despots* (2006)[6] and *Sex Lives of the Great Dictators* (1996) and even comedy recordings such as *The Collected Broadcasts of Idi Amin* (1975) by British comedian John Bird overlook the suffering of victims and gloat on the cartoonish outlandishness of dictators like Amin, as if their "lifestyles" are merely variations on those of other wealthy, powerful celebrities. Amin's time in the spotlight quickly came to an end following his grandiose claims to territory in other African countries when he launched an invasion of Tanzania. His defeat at the hands of President Julius Nyerere—the war was fashioned in personal, pugilistic terms by Amin—signaled the demise of Amin's power. He lived in exile in Libya and then Saudi Arabia until his death in 2003, though there was a failed attempt to re-establish him as president during an abortive invasion in 1989, and during his final illness there was a bid to allow his return to die in Uganda.

Such an almost cartoonish monster, a self-styled, jovial African Mohammad Ali and a terrifying African Adolf Hitler, poses a particular challenge for novelistic representation, as his reality appears to be the stuff of magical realism with a shadow of the macabre, the grotesque, the gothic, and the apocalyptic.[7] As Ngũgĩ wa Thiong'o wrote nearly two decades ago of the difficulty of finding a narrative mode to represent the outrages of neocolonial Kenya:

> A writer inhabits two places at the same time: the land of facts and that of fiction. But in a neo-colonial situation fiction seems to be more real than the absurdity of the factual world of a dictator. The world of a dictator has an element of pure fantasy. He will kill, jail, and drive hundreds into exile and imagine that he is actually loved for it. (*Moving* 157)

Peter Nazareth's *The General Is Up* (1984, 1991),[8] Giles Foden's *The Last King of Scotland* (1998), Moses Isegawa's *Snakepit* (1999, 2004),[9] and Goretti Kyomuhendo's *Waiting* (2007) are representative Ugandan dictatorship novels that employ variations of a realist mode of representation, unlike Ngũgĩ's own recent *Wizard of the Crow* (2007), though Foden's and Isegawa's novels engage with the melodramatic and sensational modes of popular adventure fiction. Written over three decades, they consider Idi Amin, his regime, and his legacy from very different perspectives, focusing on the historical figure or the devastation he caused, with the hope that he might be the last African dictator, the last self-styled King of Africa.[10] These novels consider the effects of Amin himself, his cult, and his reign of terror in different communities: the Asian-Ugandan, European expatriate, Ugandan professional middle class, and rural peasantry. They all consider the vexed question of who was responsible for Amin. The novels that tackle representation in close proximity to Amin or Amin surrogates (*The Last King of Scotland* and *Snakepit*) focus on the psychic battlefield within

Amin himself or the poisonous symbiotic relationship that develops between him and some of those close to him. Paradoxically, the greater the distance from the person of Amin in the novels' focalization in temporal and geographic terms, the more powerful is the evocation of the pervasive destruction of his dictatorship on bodies and minds, locally, nationally, and internationally. Given the sobering legacy of Amin's oppression in Uganda and the rest of Africa, all of the novels encounter a perhaps inevitable difficulty with narrative closure. This essay argues that the novels' accounts of the dictator's performances of false or invented traditionalism, distorted historiography, and bogus decolonization, as well as his media celebrity status, suggest that the spectacle of Amin has destabilized the integrity of Uganda and partly enabled a process of psychological recolonization, given that his dictatorship was fostered by colonial tropes of subservient African chiefs. The texts indicate that perhaps Amin's most heinous legacy is the reinforcement of racist stereotypes about African dependence and helplessness, as well as a propensity for a distinctly "savage" brand of African fascism. Another enduring legacy of Amin's reign that these texts represent is the suppression of Ugandan literature within the nation's schools, a problem that is only recently being addressed.[11]

*The General Is Up* concludes with a coda or delayed epigraph from Ali Shalash: "History is sometimes changed by idiots" (145). While internationally-famous, Ugandan-born novelist Peter Nazareth's novel, first published in 1984, does not name Amin as its central, idiotic general, there are many parallels from his colonial past, seizure of power when the rightful president was out of the country, obsession with the British monarchy, and belief in a divine right to govern that point to Amin. Nazareth's first novel, *In a Brown Mantle* of 1972, had anticipated the coup and the later Asian expulsion. *The General Is Up* opens with the General's paranoid reasoning for expelling "diasporic and descended Asians" in Uganda,[12] but then its perspective broadens to show the effects of this policy on members of the country's civil service, obsessed with their own careers, their clubs, their community, and their sexual conquests. It resembles a novel by Graham Greene, cited later in the novel (137), about an outpost of empire into which a gothic monster has wandered whose viciousness they initially underestimate. Their office politics are juxtaposed with the delusional motivations and power politics of the ruler who appears to recognize the advantage of operating in an atmosphere of suspicion, paranoia, and perpetual uncertainty. He is the "new conqueror" before whose "iron throne" the bureaucrats "quiver" as in Christopher Okigbo's elegy from which Nazareth takes the novel's title (Okigbo 69). As Nazareth's character Ronald D'Mello—*The General Is Up*'s author, as the novel's metafictional epilogue indicates—recognizes, "[T]he rulers had succeeded in entering the minds of the conquered" (17), a process of a type of psychological re-colonization witnessed around the world when political crises make

> the American Jew [. . .] anglicise his name and reshape his nose[, . . .] the American black [desire] to leave his family and pass for white[, . . .] the Goan to insist that he is not an Indian[, . . .] the Indian to insist he is a college graduate and not a *dukawalla*. [. . .] They were the ultimate victims. (43)

The narrative gradually constricts to the day of expulsion, and in the process characters note the similarities in the strategies of control used by the colonial and neocolonial authorities in the country. Central to these strategies is the creation of division within and between cultural, ethnic, national, and other communities and the promotion of the spectre of particularly ethnic animosity that plays on the Western stereotype about African "tribalism" as the central cause of all African problems.

The novel strongly implies that England created Idi Amin, a postcolonial Frankenstein or Frankensteinian monster. In a bid to maintain its power over the country, the colonial power enabled the General, trained in its military, to stage a coup against his socialist predecessor, failing to anticipate that the puppet would quickly discover his muscles and become a major embarrassment and liability. Neocolonial exploitation "was a game that had to be played with finesse and skill. Instead, he was bull-headed" (56). The General operates through expulsion and murder on a grand scale, but he learned to manipulate from the imperial power whose forces have been "able to deceive half the world and rake in its wealth to build up that tiny little lump of shit growing out of the Atlantic" (34), as David D'Costa thinks. The expulsion of Asians is also treated as another example of conventional imperial practices: "Wherever they went, they brought in a buffer, scapegoat middle-class, usually from another part of the empire. So when independence came, the people would be made in a thousand ways to blame these foreign scapegoats as the real cause of continued problems facing the people" (55). The expulsion itself was inspired by the British resistance to accepting its East Asian colonial subjects as citizens, the General's perverse Anglophilia, and, much later, the General's claim that his inspiration was divine. The role of all postcolonial survivors from all parts of the former common-wealth, laments D'Costa, is to be "the pallbearers for the dying British Empire" (63) and to continue to carry the freight of its legacy, though the novel indicates that divisions do arise between different communities, such as when D'Costa questions George Kapas, a Damibian, about his own commitment to the socialist policies of the previous regime. He suggests that George was devoted to merely "cocktail socialism" (93), a postcolonial version of radical chic, implying his responsibility for the General's takeover. D'Costa's departure is interpreted by George as the selfish act of a "not-yet-decolonized mind" (94).

The General is perceived in different ways by the novel's different diasporic communities, and he reinvents himself to suit his different audiences. As if to respond to some of the people's desire for a return to traditional values, for example, he bans miniskirts, and as if to satisfy the people's expectations of prophetic history, he claims to be a seer predicted in the Bible. He is by turns a Moslem, who makes alliances with General Effendi (probably Colonel Gaddafi of Libya), a supporter of his displaced predecessor, Milton Obote, a promoter of democracy, an opponent of dictatorship, as well as an apologist for the British monarchy, apartheid South Africa, and Adolf Hitler. He is described in the novel variously as "the Devil Himself," "The Grim Reaper," "a real monster," or "an honorary White Man, a leper in the ranks of the non-white people" (39, 43, 109, 44). He is either a savvy manipulator or a psychopathic idiot savant who consistently wants to "remind the people how he had saved them from dictatorship" (52). He does speak truth occasionally by accident. Intending to declare that he had taken power to "restore democracy and suppress corruption," for example, he says instead that his plan was to "destroy democracy and impress corruption" (38). Later he proclaims, "I am the government and the government is me. . . . I am the chosen one, the prophet, the representative of God!" (127).

The state of perpetual instability Amin inaugurates is illustrated by the bureaucratic limbo into which D'Costa and his family enter as their status as citizens shifts amid changing colonial and postcolonial realities. He is adrift in a Kafkaesque nightmare with elements of tragicomic farce in which at one stage he must renounce allegiance to the Queen of England as a colonial citizen and then swear allegiance to the queen as the head of state of a newly independent former colony. He must then attempt to verify his claim to be a citizen of Damibia as a member of the Asian diaspora. Nazareth extends the depiction of D'Costa's dilemma to involve the dehumanizing, ethical compromises powerless people are sometimes forced to make in impossible situations.

Nazareth's novel contains a type of self-conscious apologia for itself as an African dictatorship novel. Over and above its metafictional epilogue, there appears to be a recognition in the narrative's interrogation of postcolonial verities that the dictatorship novel is itself a generic stereotype about perceptions of Africa. The novel is both a conventionally "exotic novel about Africa" and "a work of fantasy or a draft horror film-script" as it is regarded by at least one of its naive readers, a fallible narratee (144). Its General is merely one of the ubiquitous "dictators of the banana republics" (141); he blandly claims that his coup was a "liberation from dictatorship" (101). The murder of the General near the end of the novel displays performative justice that does not exist in the historical record. Despite a number of assassination attempts and the perpetual hope that international outrage—especially post-Holocaust—would "not stand for it" (74), Amin departed only after he had almost destroyed Uganda, and the cost of his ousting—as Giles Foden and Goretti Kyomuhendo indicate in their first-person dictatorship novels about Amin—undermined the economy of Tanzania and the geopolitical stability of eastern Africa.

Unlike *The General Is Up*, which represents an Amin-like

dictator from the perspective of the General's state apparatuses, *The Last King of Scotland* (1998) by English author Giles Foden, who spent many of his formative years in different parts of Africa, enables access to Amin via a foreign interloper. Foden's novel is set shortly after the expulsion that ends Nazareth's novel. Foden's focus is the psychological and moral effect of dictatorship on the dictator's erstwhile supporters and sycophants, and it appears to echo the Western media's fascination with the psychic conundrum of the Amin complex. As in a gesture more popularly performed in films such as *The Year of Living Dangerously* (1982) and *Missing* (1982)—and Foden's novel was the basis of a much celebrated, highly successful film from 2006[13]—the intrepid Westerner ventures by accident or design or via the dictates of career into an international disaster zone and an ethical quagmire. It is a formula presumably designed to enable the Western implied reader's easy access to alien worlds. *The Last King of Scotland* dramatically supplies more direct access to Amin than *The General Is Up* and far more immediate exposure to the physical danger of anyone in his presence. However, after the initial shock of the retrospective account of an encounter with Amin, there is a lengthy delay anticipating the dreaded first meeting. The protagonist of Foden's novel then quickly becomes a kind of shadow self, double, or doppelganger of the dictator in his role as personal physician—on arrival in Uganda he feverishly dreams of himself as both devil and Christ, as one guilty of horrendous crimes, and also, quoting *Hamlet*, as "the king of infinite space" (25)—and he must save his sanity in a terrifying situation though he uses his personal danger to justify his moral inertia. He is the type of the Teflon expatriate, denying responsibility for protecting a Kenyan official tormented by Amin's soldiers in the matatu; or the Asians mistreated prior to expulsion; or Kay Amin, who dies after a botched abortion; or those, including his friend, about to be murdered in Amin's secret torture chambers; or the Israeli hostages at Entebbe airport.

*The Last King of Scotland* is a kind of latter-day *Heart of Darkness*, with a sometimes-charming monster at its center. Conrad's "blank spaces" on the map of Africa that mesmerize Marlow (a continent that for Conrad collects all the anxieties about otherness and allows a space for the existential soul-searching and handwringing of one displaced European sailor and subsequent waves of modernist interpreters) (Conrad 66) are here represented by Uganda in the grip of Amin. Foden's narrator, Nicholas Garrigan, was "mad for maps" as a boy (19), and on his arrival in Uganda on the day of Amin's coup, he recalls the Fanonian image of the outline of the continent as "a gun in a holster" (33). This Scottish doctor at the center of Foden's discursively-diverse popular novel—a well-researched,[14] highly descriptive, action-packed historical thriller, with extracts from tourist tracts, historical documents, and medical texts, and intertextual connections with Conrad—has been co-opted by Amin, relocated into somewhat luxurious surroundings in the capital, and given a generous salary and a Toyota van expropriated from an expelled Asian. Like Conrad's Marlow, who is complicit in keeping Kurtz's last words hidden from his fiancée and by extension in covering up the enterprise of greed and murder that operates in King Leopold's private colony in the Congo under cover of a grand humanitarian mission, Garrigan narrates retrospectively from a position of guilt, self-justifying frustration, or convenient moral ambiguity. Foden suggests, however, that everyone was responsible for Amin, from Amin's cronies in the civil service and expats on the make to foreign powers and international media, but particularly the former colonial overlords. Just as "[a]ll Europe contributed to the making of [Conrad's] Kurtz" (Conrad 116), so the world made Amin. The narrator conjures his memories of Amin as if he were talking to or even interrogating himself about his own responsibility, solipsistically trapped in a state of post-traumatic stress. Moreover, like Marlow in his anticipations of Kurtz, Garrigan's memory of Amin is a voice on "dictatorphone" tapes and finally on the telephone (21).

Idi Amin is represented here, as in *The General Is Up*, partly through his own extravagant, flamboyant, comically outrageous, threatening words, his fondness for hyperbole, and "his gangster sophistry" (324) that gained so much attention in Western media accounts and traded on stereotypes of the African big man. At the Ambassadors' Dinner, he is introduced with a string of titles and accolades, including "Lord of All the Beasts of the Earth and Fishes of the Sea and Conqueror of the British Empire in Africa in General and Uganda in Particular" (9). He styles himself a soldier, not a politician, the head of the national family, "the hero of all Africa" (226), Africa's "saviour" (183), "the greatest politician in the world" (200), and even the "sexual lion" who contains "all the world's fathers" (226, 152). Before the end of the first chapter, Amin boasts that he has eaten human meat, as if he has gained power from violating every taboo. The dinner unfolds after his acknowledgement of cannibalism—he will later claim he learned the practice when he was a Mau Mau prisoner (298)—and the assembled local and foreign dignitaries fall with gusto on the roast kudu. In the aftermath of the shock of Amin's declaration and his canny catering to stereotypes about Africa and Africans, the collective gorging mimics Amin's actions as if there is a collective appetite for and a sharing of responsibility for moral myopia and even for eating Uganda itself. The chapter ends with a reference to crocodiles,[15] one of Amin's favourite methods of disappearing his enemies, and later Garrigan will witness Amin extracting organs from murdered military officials.

Amin's perverse fascination works on the protagonist, who assumes a quasi-erotic power. It is "a quality of naked, visceral attraction that commanded the attention, mustering assent, over-coming resistance—fostering the loss of oneself, or so it felt, in the very modulations of his voice" (92). However, as with the young Scottish doctor's assertions that he can control wild animals like leopards, Amin's "elemental force" is associated with the animalistic, and Garrigan deludes himself that he can manage Amin, and he similarly does not question the racist stereotypes underlying his fascination. He can't shake his "deadly, addictive curiosity" regarding Amin, but despite increasing evidence of Amin's erratic violence, he continues to believe he can control his obsession (246). He has been amused and partly flattered by one particular delusion of Amin's: "Many of the Scottish people already consider me last King of the Scots. I am the first man to ask the British government to end their oppression of Scotland. If the Scots want me to be their King, I will" (111). Garrigan responds to Amin's physical breadth, his mythic force, his fondness for Scotland, and his somewhat old-fashioned, formal charm as well as his proverbial sayings. He experiences a quasi-erotic affection for Amin. He feels "[a]s if [he] were his subject" (115), or Amin's twin, and "[t]he strange idea came into [his] head that [his] body and Idi's were connected. Like the King's umbilical cord" (190).

Foden's Amin has been able to play the postcolonial card with considerable deftness, however. He calls for "African solutions to African problems" (160), and he refuses to be the puppet of the British or of any superpower. He plans to nationalize foreign businesses. Moreover, he speaks for the African diasporic community in his condemnation of slavery in the Americas, and he supports liberation movements and the rights of nations like Scotland and Ireland to independence. While clearly recognizing the fatuity of Amin's claims, Foden's protagonist is mesmerized by Amin's "wicked brilliance" (315), his "Jekyll-and-Hyde character" (316), and his always-impressive physicality even as his health declines. At the end of the novel, to a degree resembling Conrad's Marlow, but more like Francis Ford Coppola's Vietnam-war version of *Heart of Darkness* in his film *Apocalypse Now* (1979), where the Marlow character merges with the jungle as Colonel Kurtz does on first introduction, Garrigan recognizes, "I have become him," after admitting that he could contemplate murdering Amin (244). He knows that Amin is the state, the body politic, and Garrigan treats his body, afflicted, like the dictator of Ngũgĩ's *Wizard of the Crow*, with a mysterious illness.[16] Garrigan rejects syphilis as a diagnosis, settling instead for "a type of impulsive grandiose delusion that I now see might have been common to dictators" (185). Dictatorship is a viral pathogen infecting an individual but devastating a nation.

Isegawa's *Snakepit* focuses, like Nazareth's *The General Is Up*, on the Ugandan civil service, but in the period after the expulsion of Asian Ugandans and the departure of intellectuals when opportunities develop for the unscrupulous to gain fabulous wealth as "flag independence was giving way to economic independence" (6).[17] The central character, Bat Katanga, returns to his homeland after completing his degree at Cambridge to seek his fortune in the Ministry of Power and Communications. He works in close proximity to the powerful General Samson Bazooka Ondogar, who approximates Amin, and like him affects an aura of eccentricity "to impress or intimidate" (7). Bat, however, is the still—even empty—center of a novel concerned with the widespread effects of dictatorship within Uganda. It is, in Thackerayean mode, a novel without a hero, but it does have multiple centers of consciousness. The novel portrays the fatal moral compromises some are prepared to make to gain great wealth before a frenzied departure. It shows the demoralization of those swept up in or willfully entering the "snakepit" of greed, exploitation, incompetence, arbitrary brutality, terror, and chaos around Amin. Amin's regime is presented as a "national catastrophe" that engulfs everyone in widening circles around Bat and the General—their families, associates, rivals, and enemies—whose power and peril depend on Amin as the dictatorship's chaos accelerates (91). The overdetermined novel is in many ways a fast-paced, sometimes off-balance, morality play, but also, in its author's words, "an adventure story, set in the seventies . . . but with generals and intellectuals" (qtd. in Vazquez 149). The novel's dramatic confrontations between the powerful that have disastrous results for the powerless are motivated by petty jealousies. This dangerous game, ruled by the law of the gun and deftly described in scenes of graphic violence—scenes often illustrating the jarring shifts in levels of diction in the novel—is set against the great beauty of Uganda, the fabled "pearl of Africa" (196), with plentiful, restrained descriptions of water- and mountain-scapes, lush vegetation, shifting light, dramatic sunsets, and weather events.

Just as the reader can become entrapped in the novel's relentlessly hectic pace and its orgies of violence, so too the novel's characters seem to lose their ethical balance in Amin's Uganda. Isegawa's narrative strategies reinforce the notion that there can be no neutral spectatorship: all those who become voyeurs of the dictatorship are transformed. Isegawa's novel portrays the main effect of Amin's dictatorship as a collective moral debasement in which everyone is caught up, though those close to Amin have been long-schooled in the amoral use of spectacles of terror to reinforce their own and others' perception of their power. There are brief, apocryphal references to Amin's banning of miniskirts, indulging in cocaine, and collecting human heads in his fridge, but the novel mainly details the sweeping effects of individuals suspending moral judgment until sufficient wealth will allow their rapid exit from the fallen paradise, and their entrance into tropical paradises elsewhere. Bat, for example, participates in increasingly reckless manoeuvres to secure his portion of spoils resulting from the systematic rape of the country's infrastructure. His girlfriend and the mother of his daughter, Victoria, becomes a spy for the regime after she witnesses her parents brutalized and experiences the General's murderous exploitation. Thrust into the role of terrified, brutalized victim, she becomes an amoral assassin who preys upon Bat's new girlfriend, Babit, when she can no longer exploit others. Perhaps the most extreme and illustrative examples of moral debasement lie in the riots of violence and vulgarity enacted by those closest to Amin as exercises of their untouchable status. The General has a special house for "hosting orgies":

> In the middle of the night, with every guest drunk or stoned, with nothing to aim at except the trees, the whole group would go outside and start shooting at the stars. There were often Russian roulette competitions, beer-drinking contests and duels fought out in bullet proof vests. The General loved holding beer in his cheeks and spraying his guests, especially his dates or pick-ups. At other times, they all pissed in the bathtub all night long, rolled the dice at the end of the party, and the loser would be made to strip and bathe in the piss. (98)

These activities display the General's power and also ease his perpetual anxiety while reinforcing his perception of invulnerability. His power is usurped by the arrival of Robert Ashes—Isegawa's fictionalized version of the controversial historical figure Robert Astles—whom Amin promotes according to the prophecy of his alchemist. The General aims at various ways of eliminating Ashes, but he cannot anticipate the ruthlessness of Amin's new anti-corruption leader. When he is double-crossed by British businessman Alan Witherthrush of Cooper Motors, and particularly insulted at the attempt because in "Amin's Uganda . . . [p]eople died for a pancake, a kilo of sugar, for nothing" (120), Ashes abducts Kate Witherthrush and then her husband. Before burning them alive, he calls for

> the Pounder. The giant man came feeling with his free hand the weight of a metre-long pestle, smooth as an egg. The woman was held down and the man started to work on her feet. Two blows and they were gone. She fainted, frothed, and oozed all over the place. The exercise lasted barely four seconds; it was so fast that Bossman [Witherthrush] could hardly believe it had occurred. . . . In another four seconds the woman's arms were gone. Bossman soiled himself and let out a long tortured wail that would have chilled the blood of less hardened mortals. Ashes barely took notice. (121)

This extended scene of torture illustrates that Ashes's personal pride—not his greed—nurtures his extreme violence; he competes with others to perpetrate yet more macabre acts.

The nation's demoralization also belongs to a collective delusion in which the ever-present madness of the nation compels a type of magical thinking. In particular, virtually all of the characters suffer from fantasies of their own invulnerability and invincibility despite the omnipresent spectacles of arbitrary horror around them and their own private fantasies of violent death. It is as if their witness to unimaginable horror will shield them from its worst expression. Bat naively believes that he can survive due to his bureaucratic expertise and efficiency as well as his willingness to use clandestine surveillance to rule over subordinates. Even after a lengthy detention in the bureaucracy of makeshift prisons, he still believes that if he were released, he wouldn't leave the country. When he is suddenly, arbitrarily released—functioning as a pawn in the struggles between Ashes and the General—after witnessing and then participating in indiscriminate murder, he travels to England but returns to satisfy some type of vaguely defined revenge and thus helps finance his brother's dissident group. The General also thinks that he is guaranteed impunity because he helped install Amin; later he considers that his personal record of survival despite many near-disasters and his own involvement in murder "just cemented his belief in his own invincibility" (189). Victoria feels the General's "might" will protect her from any threat (218), though he is as much her tormentor as protector. Even Kate and Alan Witherthrush cannot imagine their fate, partly due to their extensive experience of previous governments' rising and falling, and having "witnessed lynchings, shoot-outs, beatings, burials, flamboyant weddings[,] . . . pleasure and pain see-sawing on an invisible, ever-changing pivot"; thus, they "at times . . . felt invincible, like gods walking among the uniformed scum and the people yearning for salvation from tyranny" (116–17). Alan Witherthrush has "been too confident of the protection of the local British Embassy . . . contacts in the British government in London; friendly generals in the Uganda army; his connections in the murky world of business; his reputation as a tough guy who not only faced down dictators but made lesser men cringe and do his will," and even the fantasy that Ashes's fear of Amin would restrain Ashes's murderous cruelty (121–22). Moreover, it is this couple's competitive challenge to his power, his private army, his reputation for unspeakable violence, and, particularly, "his feeling of infallibility" that infuriates Ashes and drives him to eliminate the couple and thus squander millions of dollars in bribes. Petty jealousy and paranoid anxiety—rather than grand political motives or even greed—generate the most extreme violence.

A perverse false traditionalism also motivates some of the excesses of the General and Bat's brother-in-law, though it also supplies a justification for deep-seated inferiority. Before marrying Bat's sister, Mafuta was the husband of a former princess of the royal line, and he willingly accepted her verbal and sexual abuse to maintain his proximity to the traditional Buganda monarchy. Only after meeting Bat's sister does he recognize that psychological inferiority compelled him to endure the parasitic relationship with the princess. As a man who resents southerners as much as intellectuals, the deeply insecure General associates his arbitrary acts of violence with the actions of the royal house of the Kabaka or King of Buganda: "I am a prince[.] . . . I can do whatever I want, I can assure you. If I want somebody's eye, I pluck it. If I want somebody's arm, I harvest it, ha-ha-ha. It is what the princes of old used to do" (98). The General's family lives in a district housing the tombs of the old monarchy, and he feels the royal connection when he drives in an entourage of luxury cars to his mansion or sits on his throne for audiences with supplicants to whom he dispenses largess or contempt. Though he appreciates the triumph of the will that power affords, he regrets the prevalent atmosphere of disdain. He envies

> the old kings . . . the loyalty of their subjects. However grotesquely they misused their power, however many people they killed, people still loved and obeyed them, ready to give their lives for them. He remembered the lines of mourners filing past the coffin, orderly tear-sodden kilometres peopled by men and women who would have braved the hottest sun or the heaviest rain just to have the chance to peek at their king for the last time. (99–100)

He is never able to overcome his feelings of inferiority and illegitimacy, due to his peasant origins and lack of education.

*Snakepit* interrogates the bogus radical politics that motivated the dictatorship's early supporters. For some of Amin's military leaders in Isegawa's novel, the dictatorship represents a legitimate postcolonial revolution with important traces of the traditional monarchy. Even those officers in the army who dislike the "reptile" Amin maintain that the possession of arbitrary power by a new elite "is what we fought for" (98). The last King of Buganda "had been in exile when Marshal Amin, King of Africa, created the new line of kings and princes now in power" (99). In this new atmosphere, no one wants to be "[a]nother sad-eyed case left behind by the revolution" (104), a member of the hopeless, exploited masses. The General wants to be "king of the lakes" (105), and even Bat, who admires Amin's ejection of "foreigners" (132), feels regal as he presides over the collapse of the nation's infrastructure and assists with the sale of its resources to foreign powers. Bat justifies his success as a consequence of the democratization of feudalism:

> He himself felt like royalty of sorts. Kingship had become democratized by money and power. Soldiers

> and the elite were the new royalty, with new rituals and hierarchies. Mimicking the princes of old by stabbing, poisoning, and burning each other in a quest for a little more power and money and prestige. (80)

Bat is surprised, nevertheless, when the Saudi businessman from whom he accepts bribes expresses a desire to appropriate all of East Africa, a re-colonization justified in his mind by the Arab roots of towns on the Swahili coast and by his inability to compete with the princes in his Saudi homeland (71). In another example of the perverse melding of self-interest and postcolonial assertions, Bat's brother Tayari rationalizes his own drunkenness as "an act of resistance" if only to display the linguistic debasement of dictatorship (77). Amin himself acknowledges the neocolonial mimicry of Africa's post-independence dictators, as he comes to fear the fate of Emperors Selassie and Bokassa. More cynically, Bat, thinking of Amin, appears to recognize historical doom at work in postcolonial Uganda:

> It was the biblical land where riches got eaten by locusts. The present did not last, the future got rancid before you touched it, blighted by the looming past: the stultification of slavery, the humiliation of colonialism, the debilitation of neo-colonialism, the raging war between capitalism and communism. The colonials, the Asians, the royals, the dictators, had all tasted the bitter truth. Amin and his cohorts knew it; they had their luggage ready. (74)

*Snakepit* has a certain ideological unwieldiness.[18] It appears to focus on the nature of evil and its roots in human fallibility, self-delusion, and pride, as well as on purely psychological drives to explain the tolerance for dictatorship and Amin's longevity. Even the anti-Amin dissidents are motivated by adrenaline and a desire for adventure, rather than a concern for social justice. Bat is released from detention through the action of a British MP, and he immediately resumes his work for the regime. Bat's brother, who becomes an expert bomb-maker for the Ugandan dissident group, was first allied with Amin's private army until a power struggle left him and the rest of his group imprisoned for a week without food. His motivation is only partly personal and fraternal revenge, and he projects a post-Amin future for himself as a spy for the new regime. Other than a few initial instances when he discusses "the personality problems of different dictators" with his astrologer (65), or converses with Ashes (242–46), Amin himself appears in the novel only at a distance. Amin is "a spectre floating on rumour" in the narrative as he is for rural villagers (131), and as a result he is, paradoxically, a more plausible presence, filtered through those around him who often seek to fashion themselves after him. Amin is a shadowy double who nevertheless requires the support of others to keep his bearings in the chaos and unreality of his own regime:

> like many tyrants, he was lonely amidst a crowd of worshippers, sycophants, wives. He needed a confidant, somebody on his level, a mirror to make the enchanted nebulous world he inhabited real, a thorn to prick him with the occasional pang of inadequacy he needed to spur him on. (112)

Ashes fills this role, as directed or foretold by Amin's chief astrologer, Dr. Ali, who also advises Bokassa and Mobutu. Ashes appears to be an amoral, affectless monster. His encounter with the stoicism of Mau Mau detainees only taught him to assess the possibility of breaking individuals through torture:

> [Ashes] kept thinking about Mau Mau women caught with guns under their robes. Two decades later, he could still see them, their immobile faces giving away nothing even after rigorous torture, dying with their secrets and ruining a perfect day, a week or month's campaign. (118)

For Ashes here as for Amin in Foden's novel, the colonial action against Mau Mau in Kenya supplied important knowledge for the project of dictatorship in Uganda.

Though not explicitly Christian, *Snakepit* contains a myriad of somewhat arbitrary Christian references, though they usually appear to indicate the "fallen" nature of life without principle, a mythological grid drained of meaning. These references may also of course indicate *Snakepit*'s author's personal knowledge and his awareness of his country's immersion in Christian doctrine and dogma. Tayari's dissident group refers to a possible Tanzanian invasion force as the "Lamb," but such Biblical references usually denote roles rather than political codes. Babit's murderers offer to deliver her head on a plate to Victoria, "a bonus as well as a warning; a bonus for its Biblical dimension: Herod's daughter receiving the head of John the Baptist; a warning to keep her quiet if things went wrong" (218). Victoria earlier has thought of herself as Mary Magdalene, as does Babit when she feels compelled to rub—though not wash—the feet of Bat's British "saviour" Damon Villeneuve (173). Upon release from detention, Bat feels like Lazarus and the prodigal son; shortly afterwards, he sees his sister lying on a bed "like a sweet cross to carry and get crucified on before entering the paradise of motherhood" (168). In the aftermath of his release, he perceives

Babit as "an open chalice," but this image prompts his "greed" to say, "Let us fuck all afternoon" (166), his psychomachia-like passion play rapidly becoming carnal. After Babit's murder and his witnessing of the horrific crime scene, he rejects an eschatology in which there is "resurrection of bodies"; instead, she becomes "a trinity" of the remembered woman, the desecrated corpse, and "the ethereal Babit, the one he wanted to see again" (224).

The reference to resurrection here offers one suggestion of what appears to be the novel's handling of the theme of suffering's purification or, rather, the annihilation of meaning amid apocalyptic conflagration. Bat's motives shift rather abruptly after his six months in detention and his own enforced participation in the murder of other detainees with a hammer, and then the brutal death of Babit. He wonders about the origins of the omnipresent violence and resolves not to seek revenge for Babit's murder: "I don't want anybody's death on my conscience" (215). After the fiasco of the trial, however, when Victoria is not murdered by outraged dissidents, Bat believes that Tayari was "not beyond salvation" (239). Far more dramatically, the General experiences an about-face when he confronts the ruin of the countryside. He has gone on tour to escape the impasse of his confrontation with Ashes in which he has felt "like some dog's dick trapped inside a bitch's pussy" (148). The further he moves from the city, the more he realizes that "government was a very thin concept. . . . He stopped several times to buy things, taking the trouble to enter the small dusty shops. . . . The goods he wanted were almost always unavailable[.] . . . There was no cooking oil, no paraffin, no food, nothing" (151). He recognizes the near collapse of state institutions like schools and hospitals, and that "the gun had risen to become . . . an integral part of the culture" in portions of the country that were now virtually state-less zones where violence, smuggling, and different regional associations ruled. He sees that empty government promises are just another nearly worthless currency. However, it is the explosion that nearly kills his wife, an event the General blames incorrectly on Ashes, that makes him confront his own mortality and recognize the catastrophe of Amin's rule. He becomes obsessed with "eternal life and Judgment Day," but he has passed beyond redemption (239). He knows he should have supported a coup against Amin, though he finally violates his own perverse code of military honour when he respects a private pact made with another officer by cutting off his own toe. He knows finally that he is "already erased from memory" even before his suicide (256).

Walter Benjamin writes in *The Origins of German Tragic Drama* that "[t]he enduring fascination of the downfall of the tyrant is rooted in the conflict between the impotence and depravity of his person, on the one hand, and, on the other, the extent to which the age was convinced of the sacrosanct power of his role" (72). At the end of *Snakepit*, amid the detritus left by a retreating dictatorship, Bat, representative of his age, acquires his old job under the new regime and feels strangely victorious. He has just returned from America and witnessed Amin's entry into pop culture as a buffoon, displaying the primarily bemused disinterest with which the West viewed the tyrant. The novel's comic—even banal—closure seems artificial and superimposed, the overall sense of national tragedy and unspoken complicity is so overwhelming.[19] In this setting, unlike in England, as Bat realizes, tragedy is not "erased and carted away into library files where it lost bite, later coming off the page like a shadow, bland in its weightlessness, almost a figment of the chronicler's imagination" (172). However, despite its assertion of history's living presence in Uganda, the novel's conclusion appears to render recent historical horrors as being easily, effortlessly shrugged off. This may be an inevitable and fully comprehensible psychological response to trauma, both historically and notionally in reading or representing trauma. Benjamin, for example, wrote of the impossibility of obtaining "an easy moral satisfaction . . . from the tyrant's end. For if the tyrant falls, not simply in his own name, as an individual, but as a ruler and in the name of mankind and history, then his fall has the quality of a judgment, in which the subject too is implicated" (72). This novel's final image of Bat as "victor" with his final dreaming thoughts given to his memory of Babit and his lust for a friend's wife ignores any responsibility for complicity and perhaps inadvertently sets the tone for the next, differently tragic stage of Ugandan history.

Goretti Kyomuhendo's spare novel *Waiting, A Novel of Uganda at War* makes no attempt to portray Amin at close hand, or to mythologize him, or to consider the colonial or other causes of his dictatorship, or to assess the outlandish representation of Amin in Western media. Instead, the novel's oral history—dialogue predominates in its evocation of somewhat fractured traditional lifeways—describes the aftermath of Amin, his legacy of instability, violence, deprivation, and chaos in Uganda and surrounding African countries shortly after his departure and the impact of this legacy on the next generation of Ugandans.[20] It is history from below, from the perspective of the powerless and, particularly, of women.[21] Kyomudendo's female characters are the first and the last to suffer in the senseless catastrophe perpetuated by a single man. They appear to be virtually stateless, receiving no direct benefits as Ugandan citizens but only enduring the economic and military fallout of power struggles in Kampala that make their already difficult lives increasingly wretched. Like Isegawa and Foden,

Kyomuhendo refers to the rumours of Amin's fridge full of human heads as well as to visits to the dictator's private quarters. Foden's Garrigan, however, encounters Amin there and facilitates his departure, but Kyomuhendo's novel merely mentions that some soldiers have removed pornographic magazines from Amin's already looted private rooms. Kyomuhendo's focus is not the aura of the dictator but the extensive collateral damage of the breakdown of the state effected on Uganda's peasantry.

The novel begins at the historical moment when Isegawa's novel ends with an extended family's immediate dread of the arrival of undisciplined soldiers, either from Amin's retreating army or those of the liberating Tanzanian armies. Terror is normalized, as the family and particularly its female members attempt to survive amid the day-to-day grind of trying to locate and prepare food for a large extended family, to search for natural remedies in the face of hospital and clinic closures, to secure their few possessions from marauding armies and termites, and to decide if and when to run from their temporary shelter on a banana plantation. The narrator's mother is in the last stages of a difficult pregnancy in this impossible situation, and just when Amin's drunken soldiers arrive looking for "women, food, and money" (37), she is in labour. What might be a sign of promise in post-Amin Uganda is yet another disaster. The soldiers murder the old woman, Kaaka, who is assisting at the delivery in the absence of a midwife, after she furiously shouts at them the reckless words of the powerless:

> Go, you beasts! I have to attend to a woman giving birth to a baby who will be more useful than you. How can you beat a woman old enough to be your great-grandmother? Do you think you can scare me? Me, who used to beat my husband until he urinated in his

> trousers? (38)

Though they don't understand her language, they fire two bullets. Her funeral is shared with the narrator, Alinda's mother, whom Kaaka attempted to save, but there is a third spectre at the gravesite: the remains of an undelivered foetus that has left Kaaka infertile over many decades, an infertility that caused her husband to end their marriage. Behind the spectre of post-dictatorship chaos lies the unequal balance of power between men and women and the weight of gendered prejudice.

The combination of the everyday and the extraordinary in Kyomuhendo's account of gender relations in post-Amin Uganda recalls the artistic assurance in the lengthy first section of Chinua Achebe's *Things Fall Apart* or Buchi Emechetta's ironically-titled *The Joys of Motherhood*, though the focus here is on the sufferings of women that have only worsened through the disaster of Amin's rule and the new helplessness of some men faced with their powerlessness before the armed soldiers and the new, mindless, testosterone-driven bravado of other men. Even in a modern war zone, however, there is time for the telling of folk tales and the origins of names, orature indicating the survival of cultural practices as forms of resistance, particularly in female communities. Nyinabarongo, for example, has been driven away by her husband's family and forced to leave behind her son after being coerced into the marriage:

> The problem started with the birth of her first child, a boy, who had presented his legs first during a difficult childbirth. That is why he was given a twin name and various rituals were performed. When she bore her second child, a daughter, she was also given a twin name because the child's two upper teeth grew before the

> lower ones. That's how Nyinabarongo got her name, meaning "mother of twins," even though her children are not really twins. (8)

We learn later that Kaaka, the woman murdered after her tirade against Amin's marauding soldiers who had an even more troubled reproductive history, had defied colonial authorities in the past when they tried to force all girls to wear manufactured dresses they couldn't afford instead of cheaper, durable calico wraps. She repeats the folk tale of the white dove with a revolutionary message that galvanized women's resistance, and the young girls recite the tale in her memory.

Faraway political tragedies, however, do impinge upon the already difficult lives of these rural women. The narrator's friend Jungu, for example, is the offspring of an exploitative, violent relationship between a poor widow and a wealthy Asian manager of a cotton mill who refuses to pay her deceased husband's wages. Jungu's ashamed mother had attempted to murder her child, but neighbours and the police rescued the baby and forced her mother to nurse it. Traditional anxieties about the suicidal tendencies of the offspring of "mixed" parentage provide Alinda with an explanation for Jungu's tragic flight after her lover in the departing Tanzanian forces, not realizing he had stayed behind to be with her. Alinda's uncle Kembo loses his job as a night watchman at a sawmill "when Idi Amin chased the Indians away from Uganda" (57), but he is coerced into becoming a Muslim through the offer of an expropriated Indian shop. His wife won't convert, and family tensions escalate until his business collapses, his newly married wives leave him, and he returns to the village with his long-suffering first wife, who also then deserts him. The woman from Zaire who is regarded as a witch by the men has gained her knowledge of herbs as an indirect result of high-level political manoeuvres: "When Patrice Lumumba was killed by the Americans in 1961, there was a lot of fighting in Zaire" (55). Though only fifteen years old and without having any schooling, she begins to assist her aunt in nursing at a hospital without medicines in Stanleyville, and she learns the uses of different plants.

Birth and rebirth in a post-dictatorship war zone—in the aftermath of the departure of a brutal tyrant, his undisciplined troops looting and murdering indiscriminately—delimit the hope remaining at the end of *Waiting*. It is, moreover, a somewhat mechanical, superimposed hope given the coming decade of post-Amin chaos. A new non-traditional family composed of pregnant women and babies, new marital partnerships, and Pan-African members from Zaire and Tanzania provides the main promise of stability and survival.[22] There is more food and the prospect of employment in the city for the family patriarch, but hope for the future rests primarily on education and a shared commitment to return to school.[23] Moreover, this future unfolds in a denuded landscape stripped bare by the liberating armies, crops and livestock replaced by landmines that blow off the leg of an old man.[24] His fate symbolizes his delayed punishment for murdering his wife, chopping up the body, and delivering the grisly remains in a sack to her parents. Amin released the man from prison for becoming a Moslem, and he is now cared for by the physically and psychologically wounded survivors. Significantly, there is virtually no reference to Amin, "that monster" (87), in the ending, as if the survivors lack the strength even to contemplate what they have survived or its cause. There is, however, time to consider the end of other dictatorships nearby: "The Lendu woman asked them [the Tanzanian soldiers] to go and liberate Zaire too, after they were finished with Uganda, and kill or chase away that dictator, Mobutu" (78). There is no appetite or energy for retribution or even for justice for Amin in the face of the daily hardships amid the wreckage left by dictatorship. While members of the family have dispersed and the wars continue just beyond the border, they no longer wait to see "[w]ould we survive this war?" but they concentrate with the enforced pragmatism of the very poor and without pause for heroic hyperbole or lamentation on how they will build the future in the face of the national economic collapse and regional instability enabled by Amin.

The muted hopefulness and fatigue at the end of *Waiting* demonstrate in particular the weight of the catastrophe wrought by Idi Amin. These four novels all represent the sweeping damage effected by Amin's dictatorship locally, nationally, regionally, and internationally, and the difficulty of representing him and the monumental scale of the disaster he caused in something approaching the dictatorship novel genre. The legacy of Amin is witnessed in the traumatized, exiled diasporic Ugandan community, the reinforcement of negative Western stereotypes about Africa and Africans, and in the rural poverty and instability in Uganda and within regional conflicts.

## NOTES

1 Samuel Decalo, in a study of the pathology of dictators, refers to Bokassa, Amin, and Equatorial Guinea's Francisco Macias Nguema as the "dictatorial triumvirate" (ix). Teodoro Nguema Obiang Mangue, the son of the present dictator of Equatorial Guinea, appears to stand in waiting to become the next "King of Equatorial Guinea" (Silverstein 3). Teodoro's father, Theodoro Obiang Nguema Mbasogo, is celebrated on state radio for being in "permanent contact with the Almighty"; the dictator empowers himself "to kill without anyone calling him to account and without

going to hell" (qtd. in Birrell 26). The country's possession of oil wealth appears to allow its dictatorship freedom from international scrutiny.

2 In October 2011, US President Barack Obama sent a letter to Congress outlining a plan to dispatch one hundred troops to Uganda who would work in an advisory capacity to destroy the Lord's Resistance Army and capture or kill Kony.

3 Foden recounts Amin's describing to the OAU his method of murdering Mau Mau suspects by strangulation (128). Amin's actions against the Mau Mau as the proxy of the colonial powers may have been Amin's major training in the deployment of the psychology and violence of terror (Robins and Post 257–58).

4 Amin was not a "one-man genocide," as Natalie Haynes describes Achilles (40), but rather a modern-day Caligula (Rush 1).

5 See Henry Kyemba's *A State of Blood*, one of a number of survivor accounts by high-level officials near the Amin regime. Kyemba recalls Amin's fondness for meeting for a drink or dinner with unsuspecting individuals he was about to have murdered. *Guardian* journalist John Fairhall, arrested in Uganda in 1972 on suspicion of being a foreign soldier, recalled particularly brutal methods of murder in Amin's makeshift jails: "the normal method of execution was by 'tapping' a man's skull with a 20 lb. hammer," in some cases with lines of detainees being forced to murder the next person in line in succession (Fairhall 209).

Uganda also became a paranoid state under Amin, as what Robert Robins and Jerrold Post diagnose as the dictator's personal "paranoid psychopathology" was reflected in the nation (262, 256–65).

6 This was the title given to the American edition of the novel, presumably to capitalize on the popular TV show *Lifestyles of the Rich and Famous*. In the introduction, Canadian novelist and artist Douglas Coupland, in an anecdotal preface, comments that the book's analysis of dictator style in home decorating—which is certainly not dictator chic—shows that the dictators are guilty of crimes against humanity and also good taste. The examination deflates the dictators' supersized egos, but its focus on a kind of grotesque camp tends to

underplay the enormity of these individuals' exploitation.

7 As Dominic Thomas writes of Congolese dramatist Sony Labou Tansi's phantasmagoric 1979 novel of dictatorship *La Vie et demie*, translated and republished as *Life and a Half* in 2011, "There is evidence of a new and original variation of the dictatorship novel, where humor, sexuality, violence, and corporeal activities inform simultaneously the world of the living and the world of the dead" (xi).

8 The first edition of the novel was published by the Writers Workshop, Calcutta, in 1984, and the "new edition" in 1991, as the "Acknowledgements" in that edition indicate. This chapter's discussion is based on the 1991 edition of Nazareth's novel.

9 *Snakepit* was first published as *Slangenkuil* by Uitgave De Bezige Bij, Amsterdam, the Netherlands, in 1999. The novel was published by Knopf in hardcover in 2004, and in paperback by Vintage International, a division of Random House, in 2005.

10 Isegawa's narrator says that *Snakepit*'s General Bazooka, acknowledging that he lacks the power of Amin, "realized that a prince was no king: he still had to take crap from his king, especially if he was a self-declared king of Africa. As a prince, he could piss on the heads of peasants, but he could not get his way all the time" (149).

11 Isegawa, in an interview with Jacqui Jones, presents the devaluation of books and reading in the Amin years, when people were focused on obtaining the bare necessities of life, as his reason for leaving Uganda (90); once outside Africa, he says in another interview, "you become African for the first time, in a sense" (Vazquez 144). One sign of the more positive attitude towards books and reading in Uganda at the present is that *Waiting* itself was drafted while Kyomuhendo was studying for an MA in Creative Writing at the University of KwaZulu-Natal in 2004–05 (Daymond 113). She also knew Peter Nazareth when she studied at the University of Iowa's International Writing Program in 1997. Kyomuhendo has been involved in FEMRITE, the Ugandan Women's Writers Association, one of whose goals is the development of Ugandan literature by women.

12 The phrase is John Scheckter's in a useful discussion of

transformational or hybrid diasporic Goan identities in Nazareth's work (83–84).

13 The film is a pared-down and slightly distorted version of the novel with a much greater emphasis on Garrigan himself (played with great authority and a certain James Bond-like rakishness by Scottish actor James McAvoy) as "our man in Uganda" and a de-emphasis on Amin (played by American actor Forest Whitaker in a much-commended, Academy Award-winning performance). Garrigan's somewhat caddish romantic and sexual interests receive greater attention in the movie, and it is Garrigan, not an African official, who has an affair with Amin's wife Kay. In addition, Garrigan is himself the victim of vicious torture. Amin is generally the more jovial, buffoonish monster of Western stereotype.

14 Foden was concerned that his research might overwhelm his novelistic intentions, though he was simultaneously aware of the self-created fictional quality of Amin himself and of the questionable uses to which a mesmerizing account of the dictator might be put. He interviewed many people associated with Amin's regime, including the notorious enabler Robert Astles, and he even attempted to interview Amin himself in Saudi Arabia. See "Bold Type: Interview with Giles Foden," www.randomhouse.com/boldtype/1298/foden/interview.html.

15 Isegawa's celebrated *Abyssinian Chronicles* (2001) audaciously begins with crocodiles, in a narrative gesture evoking a very different event concerning the narrator's father at the beginning of Laurence Sterne's *Tristram Shandy*.

16 There is speculation that Amin's peculiar cluster of symptoms and behaviors indicated the presence of syphilis, perhaps none clearer than his typically bombastic injunctions to students about promiscuity (Carlton 207), or schizophrenia or hypomania (Kiwanuka 709). The root of Amin's pathology may lie in childhood trauma, though Eric Carlton points to the theory of contingency in leadership (4) and the various tensions playing in 1970s Uganda as more significant: fascism's atavistic quest for a pre-modern ideology, the desire for modernism with a traditional face, the legacy of

Baganda despotism, and Obote's over-reliance on Amin's strong arm to maintain a one-party state. Carlton significantly underplays the effect of the colonial legacy (202–13). That Amin was both the product of the colonial creation of Uganda as well as the main cause of the nation's problems informs the collection of essays in Holger Bernt Hansen and Michael Twaddle's *Uganda Now* that begins with the assertion that in 1988 Uganda exemplified "Third World disaster" (1).

17 Isegawa's *Abyssinian Chronicles*, the author's first-published novel, a Rushdie-like family saga, national narrative, and bildungsroman, refers to the "post-Independence political elite" as a group who had gained a great deal but at a terrible cost in the manner of "hardened thieves" (121). While the novel only makes incidental references to Amin, it does point to Ugandan young people's admiration for the despot's pugilistic bravado that in its early stages fostered pride and self-assurance. He is a larger-than-life, quasi-Biblical figure who can even offer "spiritual help" (135). Isegawa credits Mahmood Mamdani's portrayal of Amin as intelligent in his *From Citizen to Refugee* (1973) for influencing his account of the dictator (Vazquez 134). In that work, Mamdani refers to Amin's Uganda as a "bottomless pit" (37), but he acknowledges Amin as an astute, tactical populist, a "masterful performer" with "the decisiveness of a tiger" (59, 60). Mamdani's later *Imperialism and Fascism in Uganda* (1983) importantly indicates popular resistance to Amin. After a brief period of popular support due to Amin's catering to different interest groups within Uganda using strategies ranging from "nationalistic chauvinism and demagogy, to petty reforms and privileges for a section of the oppressed" (55), popular resistance took hold (57, 105–06).

18 However, as Ian Kershaw explains in *The "Hitler Myth,"* the dictator and the public were locked in a system that superseded narrow ideological identification in favour of shared popular values represented by a figure of charismatic authority at its center. In Uganda, as Isegawa shows, the urban public and particularly the intelligentsia in the civil service did not so much consent to Amin's

authority as relinquish their power to consent and turned instead to the distractions of career and the growing need to concentrate on survival as the economy collapsed. However inept and chaotic he was as a leader, Amin ostensibly stood for certain common values and for the enterprise of postmodernity and postcoloniality, almost as if the people had forfeited their critical, political will until the state virtually collapsed.

19 Norman Rush addresses the disjunction between the horrific subject of Isegawa's novel and its detachment. He locates the disconnection in the novel's "often breezy, rococo prose" and its unwillingness to provide "a closer approach to Amin, to the nature of his power" (5, 6). However, he also points to moments of implausibility, such as when Bat, having experienced the horrors of detention in Amin's jails, returns first from England, and then after witnessing the effects of the brutal butchery of his wife, from America to Amin's Uganda. Andrew H. Armstrong, in an essay on Isegawa's first two novels, argues that all novels attempting to narrate a traumatic history inevitably confront a crisis of representation in terms of both language and genre (127–43).

20 Kyomuhendo has said that "as a writer, I write best about something I know" and particularly about the experiences of women who were "the traditional storytellers" ("Goretti Kyomudendo" 124). She further clarifies the circumstances that inspired the novel as well as her aims:

> I wanted to write a story that would reflect the lives of ordinary people during the Idi Amin era. These are people who were far removed from the centre of politics, the politics of things like trade embargoes, exile or even the killings. Amin was not interested in killing ordinary people—he was interested in eliminating people he perceived as enemies—politicians, lawyers, academics, judges, etc. People who were bound to oppose him and threaten his power. I wanted to focus on these people: the night watchman, the herbalist, the Post Office clerk, farmer, tailor, housewife etc. How did Idi Amin's reign of terror affect them? Did their lives change after

> he was overthrown? Could it change? What did the new regime mean for them? Most of the literature produced about Idi Amin focuses on the macro politics and I felt that the ordinary people were being written out of this particular literature, of this history. Secondly, I also wanted to show the role, importance, resilience of women during times of war. (Goretti Kyomuhendo, Director of the African Writers Trust, personal communication, January 2013).

21 Kyomunendo's focus on rural women and particularly a young woman whose independent life has yet to begin distinguishes her novel from Isegawa's *Abyssinian Chronicles*, a novel that is as much a bildungsroman as a narrative unfolding in the shadow of dictatorship.

22 Daymond maintains that the new, extended family's "transnational linguistic exchanges" are "the novel's greatest sign of hope for the future" (125). Emilia Ilieva and Lennox Odiemo-Munara consider the linguistic paradox in the novel's "mosaic community" (188): while highlighting the need for a common, rural language such as Swahili to facilitate communication between diverse linguistic communities, the novel makes clear that Swahili is associated with the divisive, draconian policies of Amin and the oppression of his soldiers (198–99).

23 The great Ugandan poet Okot p'Bitek, however, would call for an African cultural revolution in education in the face of political oppression, as he responds when asked about an earlier declaration of bitter despair: "The most striking characteristic of all African governments is that they are all without exception dictatorships which practice such ruthless discrimination as to make apartheid look tame" (100). See, too, Bernth Lindfors's "Okot's Last Blast: An Attempt at Curricular Reform in Uganda after Idi Amin" (101–09).

24 The old man is bothered by the traumatic sensation of having pains in his leg after it is amputated by the slandered but wise and compassionate Lendu woman from Zaire, and this image may embody the notion of "writing as phantom limb" in Kyomuhendo's fiction in Andrew H. Armstrong's provocative interpretation, though

he doesn't consider *Waiting*: "The narrators perform the task of creating a phantom limb that enables a 'bearing of witness' to the traumas of their protagonists" (260).

## WORKS CITED

Armstrong, Andrew H. "Narrative and the Re-co[r]ding of Cultural Memory in Moses Isegawa's *Abyssinian Chronicles* and *Snakepit*." *Journal of African Cultural Studies*, vol. 21, no. 2, 2009, pp. 127–43.

———. "Reporting from the Edge of Reality: Writing as Phantom Limb in Goretti Kyomuhendo's Fiction." *Journal of International Women's Studies*, vol. 10, no. 4, 2009, pp. 259–75.

Benjamin, Walter. *The Origin of German Tragic Drama*. Translated by John Osborne. Introduction by George Steiner. Verso, 1990.

Bird, John. *The Collected Broadcasts of Idi Amin*. Transatlantic, 1975.

Birrell, Ian. "Public Face of a Dictatorship." *The Guardian Weekly*, 11–17 Nov. 2011, pp. 25–27.

Carlton, Eric. *Faces of Despotism*. Scholar P, 1995.

Cawthorne, Nigel. *Sex Lives of the Great Dictators*. Prion, 1996.

Conrad, Joseph. *Heart of Darkness*. Ed. D. C. R. A. Goonetilleke. Broadview, 1995.

Coupland, Douglas. "Tree Forts and Love Shacks." Introduction. *Dictators' Homes*, by Peter York, Atlantic Books, 2005, pp. vii-viii.

Daymond, M. J. Afterword. *Waiting, A Novel of Uganda at War*, by Goretti Kyomuhendo, The Feminist Press, 2007, pp. 113–34.

Decalo, Samuel. *Psychoses of Power: African Personal Dictatorships*. Westview, 1989.

Fairhall, John. "Prisoner of Idi Amin: Four Days in Makindye." *The Guardian Century*, edited by Giles Foden, The Guardian, 1999, pp. 208–09.

Foden, Giles. *The Last King of Scotland*. Faber and Faber, 1998.

Hansen, Holger Bernt, and Michael Twaddle, editors. *Uganda Now: Between Decay & Development*, James Currey, 1988.

Haynes, Natalie. "Human, not hero." Review of *The Song of Achilles*, by Madeline Miller. *Guardian Weekly*, 21 Oct. 2011, p. 40.

Ilieva, Emilia, and Lennox Odiemo-Munara. "Negotiating Dislocated Identities in the Space of Post-Colonial Chaos: Goretti Kyomuhendo's *Waiting*." *Negotiating Afropolitanism: Essays on Borders and Spaces in Contemporary African Literature and Folklore*, Rodopi, 2011, pp. 183–204.

Isegawa, Moses. *Abyssinian Chronicles* [1998]. Vintage, 2001.

———. *Snakepit* [1999]. Vintage, 2005.

Jones, Jacqui. "Traversing the Abyss: Moses Isegawa: An Interview and Commentary." *English in Africa*, vol. 27, no. 2, 2000, pp. 85–102.

Kershaw, Ian. *The "Hitler Myth": Image and Reality in the Third Reich*. Oxford UP, 1987.

Kiwanuka, Semakula. *Amin and the Tragedy of Uganda*. Weltforum Verlag, 1979.

Kyemba, Henry. *A State of Blood: The Inside Story of Idi Amin*. Ace Books, 1977.

Kyomuhendo, Goretti. Interview by Stephen Gray. *Research in African Literatures*, vol. 32, no. 1, Spring 2001, pp. 123–25.

———. *Waiting, A Novel of Uganda at War*. The Feminist Press, 2007.

*The Last King of Scotland*. Directed by Kevin Macdonald. Based on the novel by Giles Foden. Fox Searchlight Pictures, DNA Films Ltd. and FilmFour, 2006.

Lindfors, Bernth. "Okot's Last Blast: An Attempt at Curricular Reform in Uganda after Idi Amin." *Long Drums and Canons: Teaching and Researching African Literatures*, Africa World P, 1995, pp. 101–09.

Mamdani, Mahmood. *From Citizen to Refugee: Uganda Asians Come To Britain*. Frances Pinter, 1973.

———. *Imperialism and Fascism in Uganda*. Heinemann Educational Books, 1983.

Nazareth, Peter. *The General Is Up*. TSAR Publications, 1991.

Ngũgĩ wa Thiong'o. *Moving the Centre: The Struggle for Cultural Freedoms*. James Currey, 1993.

———. *Wizard of the Crow*, translated by Ngũgĩ wa Thiong'o, Anchor

Books, 2007.

Okigbo, Christopher. *Labryinths with Paths of Thunder.* Africana Publishing, 1971.

Okot p'Bitek. *Africa's Cultural Revolution.* Macmillan, 1973.

Robins, Robert S., and Jerrold M. Post. *Political Paranoia: The Psychopolitics of Hatred.* Yale UP, 1997.

Rush, Norman. "The Last Word on Evil." Review of *Snakepit,* by Moses Isegawa, *The New York Review of Books,* 7 Oct. 2004, pp. 1–9.

Scheckter, John. "Peter Nazareth and the Ugandan Expulsion: Pain, Distance, Narration." *Research in African Literatures,* vol. 27, no. 2, 1996, pp. 83–93.

Silverstein, Ken. "Teodorin's World." *Foreign Policy,* Mar.-Apr. 2011, pp. 1–3.

Thomas, Dominic. "Sony Labou Tansi—The Conscience of Africa and the Voice of the People." Introduction. *Life and a Half* by Sony Labou Tansi, Indiana UP, 2011.

Vazquez, Michael C. "Hearts in Exile: A Conversation with Moses Isegawa and Mahmood Mamdani." *Transition,* vol. 10, no. 2, 2001, pp. 126–50.

York, Peter. *Dictators' Homes.* Atlantic Books, 2005.

York, Peter, and Douglas Coupland. *Dictators' Homes: Lifestyles of the World's Most Colorful Despots.* Chronicle Books, 2006.

## SNAPSHOTS

*For Peter Nazareth*

I never saw the Indians leave.

But since my eyes
Could colour the rainbow
I have seen the Indians leave.

I have intimately touched
Their exodus in the story of my land.
I saw them leave
When a man killed Archbishop Janan Luwum!

I smelt their blood
In the war of 1979
When whole villages
Lay dumb.

I see them all the time
I wish I could kneel
At my father's grave.

I see the Indians on a journey
Away from their home
In the abandoned houses
Of our districts.

In the headless body of a Tutsi woman
With a baby still on her back
Floating her way

To our lake shore
I see the Indians leave.

Everyday I think of dictators
I see the Ugandan Indians leave.

Susan Nalugwa Kiguli

# CENSORSHIP OF PUBLIC DISCOURSE IN THE EARLY YEARS OF THE AFRICAN LITERATURE ASSOCIATION‡

Bernth Lindfors

The African Literature Association (ALA) was founded as an academic organization open to all. The first draft of its Constitution, formulated in Austin at the end of its inaugural conference in the spring of 1975, stated that "it welcomes membership from all countries."[1] This language was retained in a revision of the Constitution proposed four and a half years later in the fall of 1979 and ratified at the annual conference held at the University of Florida at Gainesville in the spring of 1980.[2] There was still some dissatisfaction with the text of this revision, so an amended revision was passed unanimously the following year at the conference held at Claremont, which specified that the ALA was "open to scholars, teachers and writers from every country" and "welcomes the participation of all who produce the subject of our study and hopes for a constructive interaction between scholars and artists."[3]

However, at the business meeting at Claremont, Dennis Brutus, reporting on deliberations of the Issues Committee, "read and proposed as a resolution for ALA endorsement" a measure, earlier ratified by the United Nations, "calling for Cultural, Academic and other boycotts of South Africa" as part of "the international campaign against *apartheid*."[4] This meant terminating all links to South Africa, including any collaboration

‡ This paper was to be given at the ALA conference in 2020, which was canceled due to the COVID-19 pandemic. It appears here for the first time.

or exchanges with South Africans as well as any cooperation with them in research programs. In other words, put simply, the ALA would no longer be an academic organization open to all. South Africans were to be excluded. But this applied in practice only to those still living in their homeland. It was assumed but never explicitly stated that South Africans living in exile would be exempt from this boycott.

Before reviewing the lively controversy this resolution provoked at that time, it may be instructive to recall a similar incident that occurred just before the ALA was formed. In 1974-75 Dennis Brutus was serving as a Visiting Professor of English and Ethnic Studies at the University of Texas at Austin, a year in which two South African poets—Oswald Mtshali and Mongane Wally Serote—happened to be in the United States studying at Columbia University. This being the case, Dennis envisioned inviting them as well as other South African professors and poets currently teaching in the United States—namely, Es'kia Mphahlele, Keorapetse Kgositsile, Cosmo Pieterse, Mazisi Kunene, and Dan Kunene—to come to Austin in the spring to participate in a poetry reading on the anniversary of the Sharpeville massacre. He received encouragement from the Chairman of the University's African and Afro-American Studies and Research Center to do so and proceeded to phone them. The budget for this event was small, so he could offer to pay only their local expenses with no promise of an honorarium, but this did not matter. All of them were enthusiastic about coming and participating as a group.

Then something happened that changed this plan dramatically. In the middle of the fall, seven or eight University of Texas faculty and graduate students travelled to Chicago in my VW bus to attend the African Studies Conference, where we held a public meeting to discuss the possibility of forming an

African Literature Association in Austin on the weekend of the Sharpeville commemoration. This was approved by everyone in attendance, and we returned to Austin excitedly exchanging ideas on how to proceed. Instead of merely hosting a poetry reading, we decided to ask the College of Liberal Arts to sponsor a larger event that would bring more writers and scholars to campus for a weekend of discussions and festivities still focusing primarily on South Africa but now also involving participants from other parts of Africa as well. The Dean of Liberal Arts agreed to fund such a Symposium on Black South African Literature with input from representatives of other nations as part of the proceedings.

It was not difficult to persuade writers from West and East Africa who were based in the United States to join us, and our final program included such names as Chinua Achebe, Emmanuel Obiechina, Romanus Egudu, Pol Ndu, Biodun Jeyifo, Kofi Awoonor, Ama Ata Aidoo, Peter Nazareth, and Ali Mazrui, all of whom spoke as respondents to the keynote addresses given by the South Africans. We also allowed plenty of time for participation from the audience at each session.

Dennis meanwhile was trying to round up extra funding from foundations enabling us to invite additional writers from the African continent. He was especially interested in enlisting a few writers from South Africa, white and of color, in the proceedings. These initiatives failed, but when we learned that Nadine Gordimer would be visiting the United States in March, Dennis asked me to write her to see if she would be available. I did so on January 15th, and she cabled her acceptance as soon as she received my letter ten days later. She expressed an interest in participating in the Sharpeville commemoration by reading a portion of her latest novel, *The Conservationist*, which was about to be published on March 11th.[5]

This is when things began to go awry. In a letter I subsequently wrote to Gordimer explaining what happened, I said,

> There were no local objections to your appearance on the program either as a speaker or reader of poetry until after we received a phone call from one of the [South African] "featured speakers" ... who indicated that he and other "featured speakers" would be unwilling to share the same platform with you ... "or any other white South African." Dennis called the other featured speakers who were in the United States to verify this statement. Most of them agreed with the position but there was some difference of opinion. For example, one said he would be willing to share the platform with any white South African, even the Prime Minister; another said he would even object to white South Africans sitting in the audience and listening to the discussions. The spectrum of opinions was rather wide, but at least three of the five writers consulted were ready to pull out (or perhaps walk out) if you or any other white South African writer were to "participate."[6]

Dennis had earlier written to Gordimer claiming that at the Working Committee meeting he had spoken strongly in favor of the principle that the ALA should be open to all, but admitting that he had called for the withdrawal of her invitation to the Symposium because he thought it would be consistent with what he had said to his fellow South Africans in order to allay their dissatisfactions and anxieties.[7]

In her reply, Gordimer was quick to point out that these two principles were contradictory, making it "seem unlikely that you will succeed easily in separating racism from plain colour discrimination. … Your council has not withdrawn the invitation because I am a white racialist, but simply because I am white. Therefore my colour has remained the operating factor. I don't know how we get around that one."[8]

This contretemps was never mentioned at the Symposium or at the poetry reading commemorating Sharpeville, and not one of the five white South Africans present was harassed or prevented from speaking from the floor. Even before the Claremont meeting there were a number of South Africans who continued to participate in our conferences. A case in point was Richard Rive who was invited by Emile Snyder to appear as a keynoter at Bloomington in 1979. One of the highlights of that meeting was reported to be Rive's "spell-binding autobiographical speech" delivered at the conference dinner.[9]

After he learned of the Boycott measure adopted at Claremont, Rive wrote to me asking,

> Is it true that the ALA resolution against South African writers involves Blacks as well? Does that mean that I can no longer be a member since I am a collaborator back home (shades of ridiculousness). However, there seems to be confusion here. I am quite in favour of writers like Stephen Gray (who could not care a stuff about his fellow writers and is squeezing everything he can out of the system as a white) being 'black'balled. But how on earth can Black writers (who are having a tough time) be ostracized?[10]

In response, I told Rive, "I don't know how or even whether the new ALA resolution will be enforced at future meetings. … I can't imagine that anyone would object if someone like Fatima Dike (who attended last year's meeting [in

Claremont] and spoke out against the resolution) … or yourself were to attend and participate. In other words, it may function more as a 'whiteball' rather than a 'blackball,' though there may be a few exiles who would claim that any South African of whatever hue who is given a passport by the South African government would not be sufficiently 'opposed to the system' to be allowed to speak."[11]

In fact, at subsequent conferences we never learned from this self-appointed censorship committee, composed entirely of South African members in exile, whom they chose to exclude from participation. Perhaps they actually seldom intervened, relying on future conference conveners to do the necessary discriminatory work for them. Another possible explanation is that scholars in South Africa knew they would not be welcome at ALA meetings and decided to stay away. Before Claremont the ALA averaged about six paid-up members residing in South Africa annually. By 1984, there were only two remaining.

And meanwhile debates within the ALA were getting nastier. In March of 1985 Nancy Schmidt wrote to President Peter Nazareth resigning her position on the ALA's executive council because "this year's meeting was the culmination of 11 years of intensifying politicization of ALA by a minority of members who wish to pursue political goals which are not related to the study of literature. … Every year we are faced with attempts to censure opposing views."[12] Ex-President Emile Snyder echoed this concern in the pages of the *ALA Newsletter* when he stated that "I see nothing wrong in the linking of politics with literature, during our annual meetings, only insofar as the politics of our opinions do not silence the voices of different and even of dissenting opinions."[13]

I added to the discussion by suggesting that the

> ALA repudiate any political posture that impedes scholarship. I believe that the ALA ought to be open to anyone who wishes to join it and that members attending annual meetings ought to have the right to hear opinions from any corner of the globe. Anything else amounts to discrimination and censorship—evils that lie at the very heart of apartheid and other oppressive, coercive social structures that thwart human freedom. I also believe that there should be no boundaries placed on scholarly research; there should be no subjects, no ideas, no territories that are off limits to the researcher. Anything else restricts freedom of inquiry and predisposes the researcher to bias and error. Further, I believe that a scholar should have the right to say what he thinks to any audience without fear of prosecution, intimidation, insult or injury. Anything else is intellectual slavery, a condition in which the first and foremost freedom—freedom of speech—is extinguished.[14]

There were many others who contributed to this discussion of the ALA on its tenth anniversary, but no action was ever taken to change the ALA's boycott policy.

Then, in August 1986, I received another letter from Richard Rive announcing that he had been appointed as a visiting professor at Harvard for the spring semester of 1987 and wondering if there might be any conferences he could attend while he was in the United States. He said,

> I am not sure how welcome South Africans who choose to remain on in South Africa and fight from within are at the ALA. I was led to believe, not very welcome. But if we are, and it falls within that period, I would love to

> attend.[15]

I told him,

> I believe there would be no objection to your *attending* the ALA conference at Cornell University in April, but if you wish to participate by reading a paper, that would have to be cleared by the Executive Committee, which is currently headed by Cecil Abrahams (Bishop's University, Lennoxville, Quebec, JIM IZ7, Canada). I cannot predict how the committee might respond to such a petition. They would probably ask you to provide evidence of your opposition to apartheid and then vote on the matter. If you wish to subject yourself to this type of vetting, write to Cecil.[16]

Rive's response was brief: "There is no chance whatsoever that I shall submit my anti-apartheid record for scrutiny by those who are not part of the physical struggle."[17]

Two months later I heard from him again, this time with an interesting story to tell:

> On Monday I received a phone call from a lady at Cornell [i.e. Anne Adams] (who seemed to be the convener or top executive) who told me about the conference, hummed and hawed, and then said that Miriam Tlali had been invited as the keynote speaker, was on plenty of panels and had to address schools in the Cornell area. She wasn't coming. The Cornell lady (I think) had only *just* learned that I was in the country, *only just.* Could I stand in.
>
> My approach was cautious. She admitted that she had

> not yet consulted anyone, and was doing it on her own initiative. I reminded her of that crazy resolution about South Africans not in exile, and advised her to consult her executive and then come back to me...She said she would phone that evening.
>
> She phoned back an hour later most embarrassed. She must have phoned Pittsburg and Canada [where Brutus and Abrahams were teaching]. What she was in fact doing was disinviting me! (Shades of Nadine Gordimer!) She herself mentioned that the situation was bizarre.[18]

But bizarre as it was, this was evidence of the kind of control exerted by a few individuals (indeed, by perhaps only one person) who happened to be on the censorship committee. On this issue, he spoke for the entire membership of ALA as a whole. There appears to have been no consultation with anyone else, not even other members of the committee. Perhaps every member of that self-ordained committee had this power single-handedly to blackball anyone in South Africa. And this had the blessing of the ALA as a valid and effective contribution to ending apartheid in South Africa.

In 1994, when South Africa eventually completed its transition to full democracy, the ALA no longer needed a boycott policy, and as more South Africans started to turn up at our meetings, presumably with no interference from members of our censorship committee, we began to learn much more about what South Africans were writing as well as what they had produced during the period we could not hear directly from or about them.

There were a number of memorable moments in this new era of openness. One of the most significant was the keynote address given by Albie Sachs at the Charleston conference in

2013. We also were able to mount a successful conference in Johannesburg and increase our membership in South Africa as a consequence. One hopes the ALA will never again make the mistake of forming a censorship committee.

## NOTES

1. *ALA Newsletter*, vol. 1, no. 3, Summer 1975, p. 4.
2. See "Report of the Constitutional Revision Committee," *ALA Newsletter*, vol. 6, no. 1, Winter 1980, pp. 4-5.
3. *ALA Newsletter*, vol. 7, no. 2, Spring 1981, p. 4.
4. Ibid., p. 5. This initiative was based on "Resolution No. 206E of the United Nations as adopted on December 16, 1980 on Cultural, Academic and other boycotts of South Africa."
5. This exchange of letters, as well as many that follow, can be found in the correspondence files of *Research in African Literatures* held at the Harry Ransom Center, University of Texas at Austin.
6. Letter from Lindfors to Gordimer, March 12, 1975, Harry Ransom Center.
7. This letter from Brutus to Gordimer, January 31, 1975, is among the Gordimer papers held at the Lilly Library of Indiana University.
8. Letter from Gordimer to Brutus, February 21, 1975, Harry Ransom Center.
9. *ALA Newsletter*, vol. 5, no. 2, Spring 1979, p. 1.
10. Letter from Rive to Lindfors, November 3, 1981, Harry Ransom Center.
11. Letter from Lindfors to Rive, December 2, 1981. Harry Ransom Center.
12. Letter from Nancy Schmidt to Peter Nazareth, March 24, 1985. Harry Ransom Center.

13. Emile Snyder. "Strength and Growing Pains in the Life of a Young Association." *ALA Bulletin*, vol. 10, no. 4, Fall 1984, p. 11.
14. Bernth Lindfors. "The Trouble with the ALA." *ALA Bulletin*, vol. 10, no. 4, Fall 1984, p. 15.
15. Letter from Rive to Lindfors, August 18, 1986. Harry Ransom Center.
16. Letter from Lindfors to Rive, November 13, 1986. Harry Ransom Center.
17. Letter from Rive to Lindfors, February 5, 1987. Harry Ransom Center.
18. Letter from Rive to Lindfors, April 1, 1987. Harry Ransom Center.

# Introductory note to "New Year Trickster"

I came across Peter Nazareth's *In the Trickster Tradition* because it had been published by Bogle L'Ouverture—also the publisher of my first novel. I was intrigued by the title and by a happy coincidence had read the novels of all the three authors featured in the book. Some months later, I was forwarded a piece Peter had written about my first novel and I was put in contact with him. Subsequently, we had many discussions, by e-mail, on who or what a trickster could be. And whether a trickster could also be tricked. Was it a character or was it the text? Or was it the author who lulls you into believing a particular reality before pulling the rug from under your feet?

Peter taught me to never believe the storyteller but to always believe the story. So I narrated to him, in a series of e-mails, an allegedly true story that had bothered me for years. It was doing the rounds in Kampala in 1963 or thereabouts but some people claimed that the events had taken place in what was then "Bombay" and had had a happy ending. Others were adamant that it all ended in tears. Either way, given the glaring inconsistencies in numerous versions of the same story, Peter had suggested I write my own version.

Where facts were missing, fiction came to the rescue. And fiction often has a way of uncovering the truth…

This story was never submitted for publication. I guess it was waiting for a very special occasion.

Jameela Siddiqi

# NEW YEAR TRICKSTER

Jameela Siddiqi

Joe hated the entire ritual of forced merry-making. So what if it happens to be 31st December, 1963? It's just a number. Does the universe care whether it was 1963 or 2263? This entire ritual of staying up until midnight, dancing away, drinking away and then counting down to midnight was absurd. That dingy Goan Institute clubhouse and its lousy band. The habitual drunks at the bar with their Johnnie Walker wisdom running loud and high. All those heavily-powdered and lipsticked girls – disdainful towards the decent guys and positively drooling over the cads who drove fast cars they'd borrowed from rich friends. Then there were those who danced only with their regular boyfriends and others who danced with just about anyone. Unattached girls seated at the far end of the room. What was the point of calling them wallflowers? As far as he was concerned a flower was a flower no matter where it grew.

What really annoyed him about such events was that he never managed to muster up enough courage to ask an attractive young lady for a dance. He felt sure the answer would be 'No'. He knew he really ought to ask one of the so-called wallflowers. It would've been a gentlemanly thing to do. But he dreaded the possibility that they would say 'Yes', eagerly, and then proceed to plaster themselves all over his fragile body while leaving lipstick stains all over his neatly pressed jacket.

His friend, Solomon, had no such qualms. He just had to make an entrance to any such joint and at least a dozen dizzy things would be falling all over him: "Hey Solly! Where you been, man? You disappeared all Christmas. Now, c'mon, let's move it Solly Baby!"

How did Solly do it? He wasn't particularly good-looking and neither was he clever in any sense of the word. Lousy grades at school and then a ready-made job in the family business, a thriving second-hand furniture shop. How on earth could any young woman prefer a shop worker over a smart legal assistant? Joe not only had a much-coveted job with the town's top barrister but also had to deal directly with high class people all of whom had high-class legal wrangling going on all the time. Many of their famous battles had been famously won by Joe's boss, the famous barrister. Although Joe was no more than a general dogsbody – typing notes and briefs, answering the telephone and managing the appointments diary – he did feel close to the great and the good by virtue of being in the legal business. How could women possibly not find that glamorous?

Solly and Joe had the same argument every New Year's Eve – and, for that matter, on most Saturday nights:

"Come on, man," urged Solly. "How the hell are you going to meet nice girls if you don't come out dancing?"

"I don't feel like it. First, there won't be anyone nice and then, even if I do take to someone and she accepts my invitation to dance, she will never phone back. What's the point?" Joe would say sulkily.

"You're coming and you're going to do exactly as I say. Just watch me and do whatever I do," Solly would coax.

It was one of those unlikeliest of friendships. The brazen, butter-wouldn't-melt, overly confident Solly and timid little Joe, always overshadowed by his only friend.

Joe didn't really know too many men in his age group. He felt they were laughing at him behind his back because of his closeness to the 40-something spinster, Miss Da Costa, a senior secretary at his law firm. She was well known for her pursed lips and her general disapproval of all forms of merry-making. It was rumoured she had once been in love, many years ago and had been ditched at the altar. It was said, that from that day on, Miss Da Costa resolved to never have anything more to do with men. But, for some reason, she'd taken a shine to Joe and started showering him with all that motherly affection that had no place else to go. As a result, Joe was always very well looked after, his clothes immaculate and expertly mended, and his stores packed with endless supplies of homemade goodies like cakes, biscuits and pickles. He didn't actually live with her, but he may as well have done. She had a compact house on the outskirts of town and Joe was a regular visitor at mealtimes.

The arrangement caused all the other boys to label him "Mama's Boy" even though his own Mama had long departed from this world. Miss Da Costa would do anything for Joe: "Joe my boy, anything you want, at any time, you just come to me. No need for explanations. As long as it is legal, you know I will do anything for you."

Solly was the only young man who didn't give Joe a hard time over his emotional attachment to Miss Da Costa. He was happy to take Joe under his wing and teach him the ways of the world. And, for Solly, "world" meant young women and their multifarious nuances.

Solly always won any argument and so they arrived at the New Year's Eve ball, Solly gliding in upfront with his arms spread far and wide, ready to welcome all the giggling, simpering girls, while Joe followed close behind, dragging his heels like a schoolboy who was being march off to the dentist.

Inside the dance hall, Joe surveyed the same old scene of balloons and faded paper chains made of coloured crepe paper, leftover sheets still messily cluttered about here and there. Solly was already on the dance floor with one of the prettiest girls in the room. The band had struck up a sprightly rock 'n' roll number and Joe noted, bitterly, that it always began like this and then ended up with slower, smoochier numbers with the lights dimmed down and bodies clinging to one another as though cosied up on vertical beds. Then the lights would go off completely and the countdown to midnight would begin....

But there was a while to go yet. It was still only half past nine. What on earth was he going to do until midnight?

His eyes moved across to the tables at the back. The usual line of wallflowers in ill-fitting dresses and beehives, wistfully watching the lucky ones. Even if nobody had asked them for a dance, couldn't they at least try and look like they were enjoying chatting to one another? Where was the joy in approaching a girl for a dance if she appeared to have nothing better to do?

At that exact moment his eyes fell upon her. He had never seen her before. She was seated, alone, at one of the tables with a small bottle of Coca-Cola, twirling the straw with one hand. Most certainly alone but she didn't have the look of a wallflower. Why had he never seen her before? In a small place like this, and especially among those who frequented such dances, everyone was known to everyone else – at least by sight.

She must be from another town – or perhaps even a neighbouring country. But then, why was she alone? Surely, her hosts would've been with her? What kind of host leaves you alone having brought you to a New Year's Eve dance?

He felt his anger rising at her imagined hosts. A beautiful young girl, from another place, left alone to fend for herself among drunken strangers.

Without a second thought, he was overcome by a surge of gallantry that propelled him towards her table. On getting closer, he realised she was even more beautiful than she had seemed at a distance, albeit somewhat twee – just as he liked them –

dressed in a confection of peach taffeta and net meringue-like number that made her look like a bridesmaid.

She's much too beautiful to be alone. Her escort might've gone to the Gentlemen's Room – or perhaps he's popped out to his fancy racing car because he left his cigarettes behind?

Even if she is with someone, there is no harm in saying good evening and looking after her until the return of whoever the lucky chap happens to be.

He approached her table with an outstretched hand: "Hello, Good Evening! I'm Joe. May I have the honour of this dance… please….?" He ended somewhat lamely, having made a beautifully confident start.

To his amazement, and without so much as a-what-or-yes-thank you or hello, the meringue of peach candy floss rose and offered her hand. The band struck up an even livelier fast-tempo number that would've made it impossible to hold her closer, but they still danced, very much together.

Just my luck, he thought. Must have a word with that stupid band leader…

As though reading his mind, the band switched to a slower tempo of a Cliff Richard number. No sooner had this happened than Solly appeared from nowhere and with a cheery Hello, swept her away from Joe's arms as though she were a long-lost friend and, within moments, had danced her away from the spot where Joe remained standing, looking a bit stupid.

Joe felt his anger mounting. So, she was known to Solly. Why the hell hadn't Solly noticed her sitting all alone? Why hadn't he invited her to dance? Why did he have to come and grab her like that, without asking permission? How dare he cut in, just as the music was facilitating an opportunity to hold her closer? Bloody typical! Solly always behaved as though he were God's gift for which every woman was pining. This time, he really had gone too far.

Time whizzed away while Joe hung around, resentfully watching Solly and the unknown girl. Since he'd swept her away from Joe, Solly had not danced with anybody else. From then on, he was glued to her.

It was nearing midnight and the lights went out. The countdown began and the band prepared for its drum roll. The lights came on again, amidst much cheering, balloon-bursting and cries of Happy New Year. Everybody was kissing everybody else. Only Joe stood alone, while the others thronged around each other.

"Where is she? Where did she go?" Solly was shouting in his ear trying to make himself heard over the din.

"Who?"

"You know, her – her, the one I was dancing with."

"Oh yes, the one you so rudely swept away. How should I know where she is?"

"O come on man, you were the one who was chatting away to her and you danced with her before I did. Come on, where did she go? What's her name, anyway?"

"Ha! You mean you danced all those dances with her and she didn't even tell you her name?"

"Yes…no, I mean of course she told me her name but I've forgotten. It's on the tip of my tongue. What was it now….Sally? Rosie? Lily?"

Joe remained quiet. He was pleased she hadn't revealed her name. He wanted Solly to think he knew, but wasn't telling.

"Come on, Joe. You know her name don't you? Did she tell you where she lived?"

Joe stayed silent, now beginning to enjoy himself. It was rare for him to feel one up on his friend and he wasn't going to spoil it by admitting he hadn't a clue.

"Joe, I've got to know where she went. She's nowhere here and she's not outside. I must find her because she's got my jacket. My brand new jacket. First time I've worn it. After the last but one dance we stopped for a drink and she was shivering. So I put my jacket around her shoulders and she's gone off with it."

"Too bad," said Joe. "Let's go. The party's nearly over."

"But I've got to find her…"

"We'll find her, no worries. I know where to find her," Joe said, sounding like he'd just had a very bright idea.

"You mean she told you? I knew you must know! Who is she? What's her name? She can't be from round here. Never seen her before."

"All in good time. Tomorrow, I'll take you to her house and you can get your precious jacket back."

"You sly old thing! You mean she even told you her address? When did she tell you all that? What else did she tell you?"

"She might have told me a whole lot more if you hadn't just turned up like that and snatched her away so rudely."

"Ah, well, you know. I was just so thrilled to see her – a brand new face in this dull old place. So rude. Sorry, man."

"But I'd had quite a long chat with her before you appeared and swept her away," said Joe, spicing up his story.

"What? While you were dancing?"

"No, long before that. I'd gone over to her table and chatted to her for a quite a while before I plucked up the courage to ask her for a dance."

"What did she talk about? Anyway, who is she? Where does she live?"

"You'll see tomorrow. Just wait."

At 10:30 am. On New Year's Day, they arrived at a small house on the outskirts of town. The front door was open but the inner wire door was bolted. Joe called out: "Hello? Anyone there?"

There was a shuffling sound from within and a short dumpy woman in a floral dressing gown waddled towards the door:

"Yes? Who? What do you want so early in the day?"

"I…err…I mean we've come to see Marilyn. Is she awake – I mean is she around?" Joe stammered.

The woman's expression changed from curiosity to bewilderment: "Marilyn? Did you say Marilyn? How do you know her?"

"I …I mean, we met her at a dance last night. You know, the New Year's Eve dance at the club – you know, in town. We were all talking and dancing and then she left, without saying goodbye…"

The woman looked shocked: "Last night, did you say, last night?"

"Yes, the New Year's Eve dance…"

"And then…?"

"Like I said. She just left, she was there one minute, then gone…"

"Well, that's it then," said the woman, pursing her lips. "She must've left because she didn't want to talk to you lot. Who gave you this address?"

"She did," said Solly. "I mean, she gave it to my friend here."

The woman's eyes narrowed. "She actually told you she lived here?"

"Well, we assumed she was visiting or something. Perhaps on holiday…?"

"Too right! This is exactly where she would stay. This is her aunt's house."

"Oh, hello! Nice to meet you, Aunty." Solly was clearly

thrilled to be meeting an actual relative. "I'd seen you around but I had no idea you had such a beautiful niece…"

"Why ever not? Am I so ugly that you can't imagine any relative of mine being beautiful? Cheeky monkey!"

"So, can we please see Marilyn?"

"I don't think so." The aunt pursed her lips.

"But it's really important. She's got something of mine," Solly begged.

"What?"

"Well, she was cold so I put my jacket over her shoulders. And then when the lights went out for midnight she vanished."

"A jacket? Wait a minute." The aunt left the room for a few moments and returned with an off-white jacket.

"Is this it?"

"Yes, that's the one! But please, I do need to see Marilyn, just to thank her. It'll only take five minutes. Won't you call her, please?"

"Sorry, you can't see her."

Solly wasn't taking No for an answer.

"But why can't I see her? How long will she be staying? Can I return later to see her if it's not convenient right now?"

"She has already left."

Solly looked utterly dejected: "Already, so early? She's already gone?"

"Yes, she went very early… I'd say too early." The aunt replied with a sad expression.

"And she gave you the jacket before leaving? Did she explain how she came to have it? Did she happen to say anything about me?" Solly asked hopefully.

"No, she didn't give me the jacket. I found it."

"Where?"

"It was lying over her grave when I went to lay flowers this morning. She has been buried for over 10 years."

***

Joe returned to the small house after escorting a dazed and numb Solly back to town.

"How was he?" asked Miss Da Costa.

"Shell-shocked! But he'll live. Let him stew. I'll own up tomorrow. Serves him right. I'm glad I taught him a lesson. Thank you, Aunty, for helping me out. It was really good of you. Whenever I'm about to have some mild success with a nice girl, in he jumps. This will teach him to lay off."

"Good. Let him learn his lesson. Nobody can mess around with my Joe – not while I'm alive. Now, this girl. What happened to her? Did she just run off in the night?"

"Don't know – she just vanished. But, when midnight struck and the lights went out, there was just darkness and confusion. And then, suddenly, in all that confusion, I found her at my side: 'Could you please give this to your friend? He very kindly lent it to me. I have to go now, bye.'

"I was still looking down at the folded jacket she had put over my arm and when I looked up, she was gone. Some sixth sense told me not to tell Solly about her giving the jacket back to me. I just took some coloured paper left over from the hall decorations and quickly wrapped the jacket and hid it under my arm. The idea of scaring him came later. I'm sure Solly must've upset her by coming on too fresh. Just for that, I'm glad we punished him."

"Never mind about Solly. Now, we have to put our thinking caps on and arrange another meeting for you and this Marilyn. You're the one she really liked, I'm sure."

"I don't know how we'll do that – I wouldn't know where to begin."

"Come on, how can anyone remain hidden in a town this

size? I'll do some digging and find out who's got a young relative by the name of Marilyn…"

"But that's not even her real name – I don't know her name. In fact, I know nothing about her. I picked the name Marilyn because whenever I go to lay flowers at my mother's grave, I go past the grave of a Marilyn, who appears to have died young. 1929 – 1950, it says. I often wonder how she died so young. Anyway, I thought just in case Solly decides to go and check the graveyard, it's better to use a name that's really there. That's why I told you to say she's been buried for over ten years. Do you suppose he'll go there and check – heh-heh!" chuckled Joe. "He's in for another shock."

"Whether he does or he doesn't, it's New Year's Day and it's high time you were off to pay your respects to your dear-departed mother. I've kept a bunch of flowers all ready for you to take… Now I won't be able to join you as there's so much to do. But you will come back here for lunch, won't you? We're having roast chicken with potatoes."

"Righty-ho, Aunty, thanks for the flowers. See you lunch-time."

***

Joe felt good about himself as he walked towards the cemetery. There was a spring in his step as he thought over things. Yes, Aunty was right. Whoever the girl was, and wherever she happened to be staying in town, she was sure to turn up again. New Year's Day was usually very dull at the club but perhaps he should go over there this evening, just in case…

As he neared the graveyard he looked about stealthily, half expecting to see a bewildered Solly searching from grave to grave for a Marilyn. Well, no problem! If he was going to do that then he'd be sure to see a grave marked 'Marilyn'.

Joe smiled to himself thinking, again, he'd arranged his ruse rather neatly, down to the last detail. It always felt good to put Solly down. He may not have had Solly's winning ways with girls, but where brainpower was concerned, Joe felt he was a force to be reckoned with.

In a few minutes, he would be nearing his mother's grave. He decided to approach it from the other side so that he would go past Marilyn's grave first. He felt he owed her, big time. After having just 'used' her in this cruel fashion, he felt he should thank her in some small way. He started loosening a couple of flowers from the posy so painstakingly arranged by Miss Da Costa. It would only be right to let this Marilyn – whoever she was – have some flowers. There were never any at her grave and nobody ever seemed to visit her. It would be his way of saying thank you. After all, most people, if they help at all, only help when alive. This Marilyn had actually helped him by being dead. He felt a pang of sadness at her lost youth…

He carefully removed a couple of the flame-orange marigolds and then, just as he was about to lay them down, he was dumbfounded. He wiped the sweat from his brow, looked up and saw the trees spinning against the bright blue sky. His knees began to give way…

Soon, he had collapsed among the scented folds of a peach taffeta and net dress, arranged like a heaped meringue, over Marilyn's grave.

# ROYAL STANZAS

*For Peter Nazareth*

The message from the Queen was clear: *Please yodel,*
She wrote to the Australian singer, who
Obliged with "I Remember You"—a song
The Beatles covered in 1962
At the Star Club in Hamburg, Germany.
Her Majesty's reaction was recorded
Not only in the journals of her consort
But in the secret annals of her servants—
Attendants, footmen, maids, vase polishers,
The butler, all sealed for eternity,
Unless greed and desire for fame win out.
How does it end? *Tell them I remember you…*

———

She worked as a humanitarian
In Bosnia, and that was how we met—
At a postwar conference on the reconstruction
Of higher education in a land
Destroyed by dolts and purists. *Oh, you're married,*
She said with what I thought might be chagrin,
*So I can't love you…* The prince she came to love
Could not secure his government's consent
To marry her, and so he gave up all—
His royal title, claims, and line of succession—
To die, for love, from injuries sustained
When he was buried in an avalanche.

———

An honest cup of tea was what the bookshop
Offered its customers before the reading
Featuring writers from a foreign war,
Which was still raging in the countryside,
While car bombs regularly detonated
In crowded markets in the capital
And in the roundabouts of provincial towns.
And yet the fighting seemed so far away
To the old men and women sipping tea
Beside the fireplace, waiting for the writers,
Who were around the corner in a pub,
Drinking beer chasers. *Will you look at the time?*

---

In "Twenty Sonnets to Mary Queen of Scots,"
An homage to a poetic form imported
From Italy, the exile's truest home,
My teacher, Joseph Brodsky, made a case
For the interrogation of a royal
Consigned to history, who seemed to bear
Little connection to the matter at hand—
To wit, the failure of a love affair.
And wit is what he had to show for what
He learned in losing her: separation
Inspires more pain and poetry than love.
The falling blade was sharp enough for two.

---

On royal absolutism the blind
Poet was clear: God's will obliged elites—
The *most sensible and skillful in affairs*—
To judge a monarch's character and fitness

To lead, to exercise authority
To thwart tyrannical desire, and to
Condemn a king who would betray his people.
Only the virtuous should rule, he argued
Till England squandered its free commonwealth,
And then he turned poetry, securing
His place in literary history.
What I would give to hear such thunder now!

---

The carpenter trapped in a seminar
Of architectural historians
Remarked that blueprints were the arbiters
Of nothingness, a hacksaw was not a hammer,
And one nail might determine if the roof
Survived the hurricane gathering force
In the Gulf of Mexico, which would be named
For the first courtesan to break his heart—
A raven-haired beauty who claimed descent
From Spanish or Italian royalty,
Depending on her mood, the time of day,
And how much money he had in his pocket.

---

The royal entourage camps by the river,
Awaiting exile, death, or a glorious
Return to power and the privilege
Of granting charters to their loyal subjects,
Servants, and courtiers, who will compose
Odes to the wisdom and benevolence
Of the mad king who ordered them to flee
With none of their possessions, only keepsakes—

A lock of a beloved's hair, a brooch
Of pewter made for a princess who died young,
A silver key. The horses graze in silence.
A heron spears a river eel. Night falls.

Christopher Merrill

# PETER AT WORK

Nataša Ďurovičová

File this under no ill wind that doesn't blow some good: a few years ago, in a casual conversation with Peter and Mary in some parking lot, of the sort where professional talk slides into personal, it was clear that a health issue of Peter's was on both their mind. An opportunity arose: knowing Peter was scheduled to teach a class on "Novels by IWP Writers," I seized the moment and offered to be his amanuensis for the semester, secretly thrilled for this chance to sit in the back row and listen to the *sensei.*

Which is how it went. Twice a week for a semester I would show up, prepared with the week's reading, ready to stand before the class, only to find Peter in the room well ahead of time, tie-and-coated, relaxed, ready to go, on a novel by the Singaporean novelist and friend Christine Suchen Lim, the Kenyan novelist and friend Yvonne Owuor, the Pakistani novelist and friend H. M. Naqvi… The method was, is, always the same: open the book, read at a deliberate pace, attentively, section by section, fifty or so pages per class. The novel unfolds like a scroll: no jumping ahead. The students are usually quiet, taking notes; in response to an occasional question from Peter, an occasional hand goes up. This is an old-fashioned way of running a classroom, as instructor-centric as it is text-centric. Yet after every class meeting, I, instructor-turned-student, find myself tuned up, amused, surprised, my book more scribbled-up in the margin than I normally tolerate; some of the papers he lets me read once the course is over are solid little gems.

For Peter reads the text closely—as the writer he is, he

parses a sentence or a phrase with the best of them—but really, he is there for the characters, caught in the force of circumstances—aka plot—in ways the kids may or may not be able to see. If he goes slow, it is so that the students, who haven't had the advantage of a life of headwinds, exile, migration, plain old outsidership, can think through the contradictions in their own way: call it ethics.

The characters that get special attention from Peter, though, are those who know how to change, adapt, move forward. What one must know to do when ground shifts underneath. Resilience is a dexterous body with a stable moral core. Staying yourself while becoming different: what the dialectician and the trickster know to do; also what a twin makes possible.

For Peter of course has a twin, if not an identical one. Mary's ying to Peter's yang is the core around which their immediate family orbits, then his vast extended family, surrounded by us, his friends-colleagues-students, in turn radiating out to the hundreds of writer friends, living on wherever in the world, but also in the remarkable joint Nazareth memory bank, and in the medium of Peter's stories.[§]

May we get to listen to them for a long, long time to come.

Iowa City, April 2020

[§] Always with a Mary footnote.

# MEMORIES IN HONOR OF PETER NAZARETH: A COLLAGE

Sandra Barkan

Gathering together my memories of Peter is not linear. It is true that there is a beginning and a present, but for the rest, it is a collage. My memories of Peter date back to 1974, though it is possible we met earlier. Peter returned to Uganda, after receiving his Master's degree equivalent at the University of Leeds, in 1965, I believe. My husband Joel and I arrived in Kampala in July 1966, Joel to conduct doctoral research, me to be an African Studies Master's student at Makerere University. David Cook was my African literatures professor; David Cook had also been Peter's African literatures professor, and the professor of Peter's good friend, the now famous Kenyan writer Ngũgĩ wa Thiong'o. Our paths may have crossed then, but probably not because Peter wasn't on campus; he had a senior position in the government's Ministry of Finance. My first memory goes back to a gathering hosted by Peter and Mary in their small apartment in the Mayflower, the University of Iowa building housing the International Writing Program participants, and where the Nazareths lived with their daughters and the girls' grandmother. Comfortably socializing, along with the Nazareth family, were several writers from around the world, who lived on the top floor of the Mayflower. It was a small, but welcoming, warm and interesting space. What followed were years of meeting with the IWP writers, readings, followed by questions where Peter could always be counted on to talk a bit and to ask a perceptive question, not infrequently the first question. The talking and the questions were laced with Peter's favorite writers, like Ishmael Reed, Joseph Conrad and Ngũgĩ wa Thiong'o.

But Peter's interests were much broader than that. To meet him on the stairs of the English and Philosophy Building was often to lead to a long discussion about Elvis Presley and twinning, or comic books, or tricksters, or the ways in which Goans were similar to Jews, or why Peter would not be returning to Uganda. Why Elvis Presley? Like Jimmy Rogers, Presley arrived in the student halls at Makerere, without context, American music to enjoy. And Peter enjoyed it and absorbed it. And Peter's shelves today are full of music. What parallels could be drawn between Jews and Goans? Like the Jewish mythical character the wandering Jew, fated to wander the earth, one also spoke of the wandering Goan, Peter claimed, the Goan in Uganda and in the US, and otherwise dispersed throughout the world. Why not return to Uganda? That was complicated and linked to the Asians being forced out of Uganda. And though I have boiled these reflections down to a paragraph, the staircase discussions were actually long and complex. Not surprisingly, Peter's thoughts on Elvis led to a popular course at the university and a book. Conrad was also, not surprisingly, a course.

And the discussions on the staircase and elsewhere also reflected Peter's broad and deep interest in literature, the works of IWP participants and so many more from all over the world. But, of course, Peter wrote about Goans in Uganda, and Ugandan politics, and about Goan literature, and the Singapore writer Edwin Thumboo, and the writer Bessie Head from Botswana with whom he had a challenging relationship, and who we discussed many times; and early in his career he even wrote about D. H. Lawrence and Jean Anouilh. And he wrote radio plays along with his novels and literary criticism. And he enjoyed teaching, and telling me about students he felt were writing creative, interesting papers. Peter was an enthusiastic teacher and mentor, and I benefited from that quality as I wrote my doctoral dissertation at Iowa.

As a student himself, at Makerere, Peter played a significant role editing and writing for student literary publications, widely accepted by the African students; and once he was in the United States, he was recognized as a leading figure in the African literatures community, joining the African Literature Association when it was formed in 1975, then serving as the ALA's tenth president in 1985, and to this day, though he stopped coming to ALA meetings a long time ago, he remains widely respected in the African literatures community. I rarely go to a meeting where his name doesn't come up in one context or another. If my memories of Peter are substantially linked to him as an African writer and critic, Peter lived a parallel life as a Goan writer and critic, so that while talking to Peter there would suddenly be a reference to work he was doing on a Goan anthology or other Goan work. There was always the African Peter and the Goan Peter, separate but harmoniously blended and always tied to literature.

All of the layers of Peter are wrapped in his family. Peter and Mary worked together, supported each other, and brought up two daughters who thrived in the multi-cultural, multi-national world of their parents. It is a close-knit family. Ultimately, perhaps what describes Peter best for me is that he enjoys sharing a glass of wine, and he carries a small bottle of hot sauce in his pocket. He is a generous, caring person, but always spicy, and frequently surprising, a happy mixture.

## TERBUANG

*Buat Mary & Peter Nazareth*

Kau pernah terpaksa keluar dari Uganda
tika Idi Amin mengusir orang-orang Asia
walau kau diizin menetap
tapi si jeneral mabuk darah
bagaimana akan kaupercayai janji diktator?

Sekelip mata keluargamu terpisah-pisah
sekelip mata kau terbuang dari tanah air tercinta.

Tanpa wang, kedudukan, pertalian, penaja,
hanya novel *In a Brown Mantle* tiketmu ke luar negara
menjadi ahli zamil di Universiti Yale
Januari 1973, kautatapi Uganda buat kali terakhir.

Betapa sukar memulakan kehidupan baharu
bila sejarah berdarah & trauma menghantu
sakitmu memanjang, bentan, memusar kepedihan,
hingga *The General Is Up* kaulahirkan
pecahlah empangan persoalan, trauma,
rasa sedih, marah, terbuang yang membusa
mencari tanah tumpah darahmu yang hilang
memahami kezaliman, kekejaman,
bahawa berbeza keturunan menjadikan kau terbuang
bahawa cinta mendalam tetap menjadikan kau kambing hitam.

Tapi tidak pernah kauhilang Uganda, Tanzania, Afrika,
meski 1974, kau bermukim di Iowa
melibati IWP/Program Penulisan Antarabangsa

# EXILED

*For Mary & Peter Nazareth*

You're once compelled to leave Uganda
when Idi Amin expelled the Asians
though they allowed you to stay
but the general was bloodthirsty
could you believe a dictator's promise?

In a twinkling, your family was separated, dispersed,
in a twinkling, you're exiled from the homeland you loved.

Without money, position, relatives, sponsors,
your only way out, your novel, *In A Brown Mantle*
making you a fellow at the University of Yale
January 1973, you bid Uganda your last farewell.

How difficult it was to begin life anew
when the bloodied history & trauma haunted you
like a prolonged, relapsed illness, swirling sorrows,
until *The General Is Up* you exorcised
demolishing dams of questions, trauma,
the unbridled feelings of sadness, anger, exiled,
in search of your lost homeland
in making sense of the oppression, brutality,
that a different ethnicity made you an exile
that you're the scapegoat, despite your deep love.

But you've never lost Uganda, Tanzania, Africa,
though by 1974, you're domiciled in Iowa
deeply involved in the IWP

mengajar sastera Inggeris, Afrika-Amerika, Dunia Ketiga,
mencari kebersamaan kita dalam kursus Elvis
mencari persaudaraan dalam pelbagai penulis.

Terbuang dari Uganda
kau merumahi IWP, Universiti Iowa
membawa seluruh dunia ke Midwest Amerika
kerana tanah airmu adalah rasa ihsan, kasih,
budaya & bahasamu adalah sastera, seni,
& penulis yang kauramahi, kesani,
adalah keluarga & sahabatmu di Uganda
yang tidak lagi kautemui.

Mary & Peter
kezaliman itu tidak berwarna
tidak beragama, tidak bernegara,
Idi Amin atau sesiapa hanyalah diktator
beredar mengikut masa
tapi ketulusanmu & keterbukaan jiwa
keikhlasanmu yang santun menerima
tidak pernah menjadikan kau kambing hitam
tidak pernah menjadikan kau orang luar
tidak pernah menjadikan kau pendatang
& di hati yang kauakrabi, sayang,
selamanya
tidak pernah kau terbuang.

Rasiah Halil

teaching literature: English, African-American, Third World,
searching for our shared humanity in your course on Elvis
searching for kinship amongst the writers you meet.

Exiled from Uganda
you made a home in IWP, the University of Iowa
bringing the world to the Midwest of America
for your homeland is your compassion, affection,
your culture & language are literature & the arts,
& the writers you befriended, influenced,
are your family & friends in Uganda
that you could no longer meet.

Mary & Peter
oppression has no colour
no creed, no country,
Idi Amin or whoever are mere dictators
ejected in the cycle of time
but your honesty & openheartedness
your sincerity in kindly accepting others
will never make you a scapegoat
will never make you an outsider
will never make you a foreigner
& in the hearts of those you're close to, love,
forever
you will never be exiled.

Original Malay poem translated to English by the poet.
Published in *Nyanyian Si Anak Dagang (Songs of the Outsider)* 2013.

# TWO IRISH POEMS FOR THE GOAN NOVELIST

Thomas McCarthy

What I first loved about the attractive and complex Goan novelist and scholar, Peter Nazareth, was that he had created fictional characters for whom exile offered no release from history. Exile, for the main character in his seminal novel *In a Brown Mantle*, offers nothing but further humiliation and disintegration, where the coinage of his native land generates heat from the gas-meter in London but cannot purchase bread. Nazareth's fictional coinage, I understood immediately, was a metaphor for un-translatable and non-transferrable national and ethnic experiences. Coming from Ireland to Iowa City in 1978, still besotted by James Joyce's *Portrait of the Artist as a Young Man*, I was thrilled and challenged to meet a novelist who had created an anti-hero of exile, an anti-Joycean, out of African materials. In Joyce's novel as Stephen Dedalus prepares to depart from Ireland, he watches his devout Catholic mother: *She prays now, she says, that I may learn in my own life and away from home and friends what the heart is and what it feels. Amen. So be it. Welcome, O life! I go to encounter for the millionth time the reality of experience and to forge in the smithy of my soul the uncreated conscience of my race.* But Nazareth's Deogratius D'Souza, whose very Christian name is full of irony as he has little to be grateful for, is more blunt and hopeless when he goes into exile: *"Goodbye, Mother Africa," I said, as the plane lifted off. "Your bastard son loved you."* In this novel and its sequel, *The General is Up*, Nazareth forged literary monuments from the cauldron of multi-racial East Africa, a territory seething with needs and fears, a potentially wealthy and beautiful landscape that was ruined by a myriad of competing interests,

Tanzanian, Sudanese, Israeli, British and American. In so many ways Nazareth's two novels have created the cenotaph around which East African Asian memory coheres. In this world of the exiled where the sense of nationhood is always nebulous and unsatisfactory, these Nazareth novels are where intellectual Goans should come to pray, as the intellectual Irish always need to light a candle at the altar of Joyce.

That nearly seventy thousand East African Asians were used as scapegoats in this political theatre was one of the consequences of African tension and British Imperial population flux and exploitation across the Indian Ocean. Peter Nazareth's two novels now survive as the most important witness documents of this extraordinary moment in African and Goan history. Deo D'Souza is our displaced Everyman, a pilgrim in that long pilgrimage of collapsing empires who makes a counter-Conradian journey to the metropolis. Nazareth has made demanding political art out of Idi Amin's Uganda, following in the technical political tradition of Conrad, Greene, Achebe and Ngũgĩ wa' Thiong'o – rather than the private Thomist, Walter Pater-like aesthetic of James Joyce. That his aesthetic was non-Joycean fascinated me when we met in 1978 and inspired me to turn to political prose, as well as political poetry, by the mid-Eighties and early Nineties. Under his Goan inspiration, I published two political Irish novels, *Without Power* and *Asya and Christine*. I wrote a third, *Without Memory*, but didn't publish it: the project's moment had passed and it had grown too old in my hands. This can happen when the material is political. A change of politics can alter the impact, meaning, and even necessity of works of fiction in a radical way that never occurs with poetry. It is the lyric aesthetic, the internal music, that always saves poetry. But all through the Eighties, I was still writing my political poems. I dedicated one to Peter Nazareth –

a poem about a Socialist health minister in Ireland, Dr. Noel Browne, who had been brought up in an orphanage, yet survived to lead the Irish campaign to eradicate tuberculosis in the 1950s. I thought that Browne was a character Peter Nazareth might have invented for Africa:

## THE HEALTH MINISTER

*for Peter Nazareth*

Some who held Ministries were honest, even holy:
The Health Minister, for example, with his miniscule voice,
(as if poverty had taken its breath away)
His hand stretched over the tenements of the ugly,
The poor and tubercular.
His plans rode through the landscape of suffering
To deposit succour, hospitals, the balsam of care.

Not a great poem, by any means, but sincerely written. And at least a good Irish minister was remembered. That August, 2003, Peter had suddenly written to me from his home in Coralville, Iowa:

"Tom, Idi Amin is dead. . . . Is he dead? Is he up?"

That same day, Peter did nine different radio interviews across Canada, from Ottawa to St. John's, from Calgary to Vancouver. How many million Canadians heard a Goan voice for the first time, I wonder, explaining tyranny, expulsion, exile and empire? The tyrant was dead. The creator of Deo D'Souza and David D'Costa had survived him, as had most of the victims of The Expulsion, those blameless people: 'Goan by race, British by education, and African by experience and commitment.' *The General is Up* would be published by Calcutta Writers' Workshop (Kolkata, 1984) and re-published in Toronto in the early Nineties. The tyrant had caused Peter Nazareth, when Senior Finance Officer in the Uganda Ministry of Finance, along with his colleagues, to be admonished by an official from the IMF who demanded to know why so much money was being spent on arms purchases. Go tell the General, as the officials replied: How can mice admonish the cat? The scandalous fact was that Uganda was not only beautiful but potentially prosperous and self-reliant. Even as late as 1982 Uganda's 'defense' expenditure was estimated at $94 million, about the same amount as the National Deficit. Here was a country that was producing over five million metric tons of cassava and plantain, over half a million metric tons of sweet potato and sugar cane, as well as vast exports of copper, tin and other metals. Corruption, of course, breeds inefficiencies – corruption such as the American Gerry Kern practiced in *The General is Up*, offering the Damibian Minister of Public Information a wide-screen TV from Germany and a 'one-per-cent cut.' Corruption brings a bed made from gold to the corrupt leader Gombe-Kukwaya; though inefficiency of a kind also brings torture and death to the government contact of a fleeing British journalist.

But back to 1978. Those days of Iowa seminars and endless cups of *Typhoo* tea in the Autumn of 1978 have a glow that is youthful, intense and passionate. How many times did I sit in Peter and Mary's apartment on North Dubuque Street, discussing tyranny and literature with Peter and Sahar Khalifeh, the Palestinan writer, or with 'Partha,' the wonderful R. Parthasarathy who had just published *Rough Passage* with Oxford University Press in New Delhi? The book was his farewell to the

English language, a long poem with the propulsion and energy of Yevtushenko's *Zima Junction.* Partha had decided to reject the English tongue and write in his native Tamil. That was an interesting, vital cultural moment in world culture, those years after the American withdrawal from Asia and before the ascent of the new China: in Ireland the poet Michael Hartnett had published his *Farewell to English* and would write only in his native Gaelic; Alfred Yuson of the Philippines had decided to abandon English and write only in Tagalog. It was a moment of unusual ethnic self-confidence and assertion. All the while in that apartment on North Dubuque Street Mary and Peter and I shared our own remnants of Empire, a taste for English-blended teas, a taste for *Marmite*, a knowledge of Lonny Donegan and Skiffle music; and an understanding of the centrality of the University of Leeds, with the legendary and cranky Yeats scholar A. Norman Jeffares. There Peter had done his post-graduate work on African writing. The University of Leeds was, by the mid-Sixties, both clearinghouse and stock-exchange of all Anglophone African writing. Leeds in those days of Harold Wilson's inflationary government was a centre of poetry and soccer.

Peter had first arrived in the United States, on a temporary British passport, as a Lustman Fellow at Yale University. He had not so much fled as eased out of Uganda on the strength of his highly original and pioneering political novel that had been published by the prestigious East African Literature Bureau. The EALB was a creative entity funded by the governments of Kenya, Tanzania and Uganda; itself a kind of beacon of hope, a sign that the creative life of East Africa had begun to flourish. So it is important to recognise that his first prophetic novel of exile is actually the product of Africa, which is why it has that extraordinary double focus of both African life and life as Exile.

Though it had been over four years since Nazareth had distanced himself from the pathological politics of Idi Amin, he was still, in 1978 when I first met him, psychologically in flight mode, displaying all the anxieties of a stateless intellectual. The recent past had been bad for all Ugandan Goans, and the future looked even worse. Mary Nazareth seemed calm and settled in her well-bred Catholic manner, but Peter was certainly not settled – he was like James Joyce in Trieste, pacing the floor, scrambling for documents, haunted by Goan history and the existential ambiguities of an Asian life in East Africa. I kept thinking that the two of them in their ground-floor apartment in the bleak Mayflower Building were James Joyce and Nora Barnacle, marooned in a territory that could never understand their astonishing experiences. Peter intended to remember everything. He wished to forget nothing, in that grand Joycean manner of an intellectual who has been outraged by historic unfairness. Amin had focused his tyrannical hatred on African Asians just as Hitler had focused his attention on the Central European Jews. One of the other regulars at Mary's tea-table was Sahar Khalifeh, the Palestinian fiction writer. I remember how difficult it was to discuss the Jewish Holocaust with Sahar, she had been so badly wounded by Israel, she said. She was also one of that day's pilgrim people. But Sahar had had to carry a double burden, a sexual as well as a racial one. Her husband had beaten her when he discovered that she had dared to write: as a woman she was not expected to have intellectual pretensions. One day while her husband was away, she had fled with her children and moved through Israeli-occupied territory. Israeli troops detained her and her manuscripts were confiscated. Soldiers became her second tormentors. Eventually she reached Tel Aviv, then Cairo, then the International Writing Program.

These stories of exile and displacement gave Peter and

Mary's apartment the character of a UN relief station, a refugee hospital, a field dressing-station where personal and political rages and humiliations were soothed by Mary's sanguinity and tolerance. It was in that atmosphere, in that apartment, that Peter was already at work on *The General is Up* as well as preparing lectures and editing crucial editions such as *Pacific Moana Quarterly*'s *African Writing Today* with its new work by Atukwei Okai and Miriam Tlali. That year at Iowa, 1978, the Ghanian, Atukwei Okai, was a lightning-rod, a passionate socialist and idealogue. At his reading of his poems and a long discussion of African poetry he said he believed completely in the necessity of social relevance in literature. He didn't see a justification for private poetry, for mere aesthetic exercises or challenges, when there were urgent matters of political and social justice yet to be settled in Africa. His themes were wonderful, but I felt his technique was poor; yet there was within him a marvellous rage to name the new territories of pan-African Nationalism. Peter Nazareth kept his council during our early exchanges, listening, interviewing, sometimes goading the politically sincere with technical, craft questions about writing. Listening to Okai, then, I felt that African writers were still at the propagandist stage of their writing, very like the Irish poets of the Celtic Twilight in the late Nineteenth Century. There was a lot of talk about the insanity of the West; not just insensitivity but insanity. The African writers cited the Guyana massacre as an example of this insanity, a bizarre incident where eight hundred Americans were forced into a mass suicide by leaders of a charismatic Christian "People's Temple" cult. A Democratic Irish-American congressman from California, Leo Ryan, and others were murdered just before the mass suicide. This, along with the revelations about American bombing of Cambodia and support for the Somoza regime, was seen by many participants in the IWP as part of the corrupt insanity of the West. Those were certainly heady times, full of political passion and chaos, despite the absence of Facebook, Twitter and Instagram. How passionate life could be, how angry, despite the fact that we relied entirely on the printed page!

In mid-December of that year our anger spilled over in a ferocious row at an IWP Seminar. Miriam Tlali, the Black South African writer, read her marvellous story. In fact, it was a young Program translator of German, Jonathan Jordahl, who read the story brilliantly. The high point of Mariam's story was a sexual encounter between a Black woman on her way back to a homeland and a guard or official of colour. The scene was drawn brilliantly, so that the reader was drawn into a possible rape scene which actually became a more intimate seduction. The woman who was the victim became a passive but very nearly culpable participant in the sexual act. If written by a man it would have seemed wrong at every level. It was a tricky incident that Tlali described; it could only have been delineated by a woman. It was an immensely complex story, slowly and atmospherically unfolding, with a spine-chilling Nazi South African apartheid aura. It was a train journey through Afrikaaner territory, with its very subtlety, its humanity, its understatement as its greatest strength. This provocative strength gave it a powerful propaganda value. I felt that it would be a thorn in the side of the malignant South African body politic. But the other African writers couldn't see this; they couldn't see any value in its ambiguity – the very element that gave it literary power. They were furious with Miriam, who sat patiently and timidly near Jonathan Jordahl. Okai in particular felt that it was an insult to African women. African women, he claimed, would not have sex willingly with a white man or a man of colour. This was too much for me. "For God's sake, Okai," I said, "who are you kidding? That's part of the story's subtlety." Okai replied that subtlety was a luxury that bourgeois writers from Ireland, from Western Europe, could indulge in. In Africa there was no room for subtlety. "Okai," I said, "that's bullshit." Uproar ensued, a flashpoint between aesthetics and politics had been reached. I reminded my detractors that in several countries writers could be jailed for merely being personal, for not being one-dimensional creatures. Our loud discussion went on like that for some time, until Paul Engle intervened with a big Paul guffaw and a few serene words. It was all part of the intensity of the moment, the intensity of our own youth. But coming from Europe where the Eastern half of our continent was still ruled by a tyrannical, systematic Communism that controlled both body and mind, I could never accept that writers should conform to any political imperative, however just. What writers should do was beg to disagree, to catalogue their disagreements, to accumulate facts, to speak directly to power. Or to ignore power, to be personal, to write only of love in the manner of Cavafy or Robert Graves, as if love was the only thing in their world. No, after Joyce's exile and Beckett's odd-ball triumphs, no Irish writer would accept instructions from any area of politics. I remember when I returned back to Ireland in the 1980s, I read in the newspapers that the Communist government of Hungary had banned typewriters. In the Communist future of Hungary only those with a license could own a typewriter. More than ever, I thought, the world needs Miriam Tlali. Three years after our savage disagreements at the IWP seminar, Peter Nazareth quietly published the story 'Just the Two of Us' in his African edition of *Pacific Moana Quarterly*.

Which brings me to this second poem I dedicated to Peter Nazareth, a poem I wrote in 2010 that I may not have sent to him. What I always love about Peter is his personal integrity, his moral clarity; as well as that marvellously complex education in Literature and Economics that he obtained at Makerere University College in Kampala, with a second degree awarded and verified through the University of London; and then on to Leeds University in its Commonwealth heyday. His education was that of a distinguished diplomat operating across the breadth of the British Commonwealth, but his literary gift has made him the plenipotentiary of an immortal kingdom of the written word. Truth is, he represents no one country: he represents all of us. Each writer creates pictures from fragments, this is the writer' task – as Camus put it in *The Rebel*: We resist the real while conferring unity upon it. All writers are ultimately stateless; in the deepest sense of their personal being writers belong to an imagined territory. Even a novelist as intellectual and scholarly as Nazareth still carries a fragmentary citizenship – belonging always to that elsewhere of the imagination. The best writers are emotionally as well as politically de-colonised; it's not that their heart is elsewhere, it's just that the heart settles in the interim island of creativity. So here is my second poem, from that second island of creativity whose citizenship we share. This is very much a poem for Peter Nazareth alone, being mindful of exile, mindful of the exile's sense of ambiguity; and mindful too of the exile's inability ever to really return. I wrote it when I re-read *The General is Up*, being impressed all over again by the urgency of that document and all of its cohering fragments. We can never go back because not only has our native place changed but we in our cosmopolitan exile have been utterly transformed. As a writer, Peter Nazareth has made all these fragments of his exile cohere. Here, then, is a long-distance salute to a master story-teller out of Africa; to a fellow writer, of course, but to a man whose work has all the urgency and necessity of great art:

# AN EXILED POET

*for Peter Nazareth*

Let's be mindful that we feel at home in two countries
And live in the one as if the other didn't exist,

Though the other keeps nagging like a second childhood.
A country knocks at the door, wanting more food,

The way an orphan might implore us. Each refugee
Flees from a country that keeps following, a country

That doesn't want to go home. Here we are,
On an indifferent verandah without visible scars:

Our first country keeps banging on the stained glass
Window, the one erected in honour of peace,

While we cower at the table farthest from the door.
In here suffering is meaningful and our dinner

Is mindful of the burdens outside. Here, food
Is assertive but gives no offence. Waiters are shrewd

In this second country, they invite us to reframe
Our pain; to inhabit just one island nation

Where the void in dinner plates is alert and reciprocal,
Where the ways are kind and the myths are mindful.

Thomas McCarthy

# PETER NAZARETH: FRIEND & CRITIC

Suchen Christine Lim

I first heard of Professor Peter Nazareth when he published a review of my novel *Gift From The Gods* in *World Literature Today* in 1991. At the time I was a young writer and ignorant of his literary connections with several major Singapore poets and novelists, like Singapore poet Edwin Thumboo. Over the years Professor Nazareth, whom I had never met, followed my writing with critiques of two of my novels, *A Bit Of Earth* and *Fistful Of Colours,* which gave me a lot of encouragement to continue my writing journey. It was not till in late 1996 when I went to Iowa City for the International Writers' Program that I met him in person one wintry midnight on the steps of the old Mayflower Residential Hall. He and Mary, his wife, welcomed me warmly as I emerged from a black limousine hearse. My first trip to the US, and a black hearse had ferried me from the airport in Cedar Rapids to Iowa City that dark snowy midnight! All sorts of Chinese superstitions about death and corpses raced through my head. But these apprehensions were swiftly dispelled when Peter Nazareth grasped my freezing cold hands as he greeted me on the steps of the residential hall as though I was his special guest. His very warm welcome as though I were his equal took me by surprise, for I was still unable to regard myself as a writer after writing three novels.

The University of Iowa's International Writing Program (IWP) was my first overseas writing residency and my first exposure to American critics and international writers. Peter's friendship and Mary's warm hospitality during my four months' stay bolstered my self-confidence. During dinners in his house with other international writers, there were wide-ranging discussions about writing, literature, and Elvis Presley often late into the night. Looking back to those nights, I believe the seed of a writing self was sown in me. These discussions were thoroughly enjoyable and an eye-opener, not only because of the wine and music but also because of their novelty to a woman writer, whose family did not approve of her writing, and who came from a pragmatic island nation whose first Prime Minister had declared that 'poetry was a luxury we could not afford.'

The Singapore government's pragmatism and emphasis on commerce, science, and technology had filtered down to its institutions. From the 1960s to the 1990s, the literary works of Singapore writers were like poor Cinderella consigned to the kitchen by the local reading population, especially the literature teachers in schools. During one of our lengthy conversations at night, Peter mentioned his hope that external foreign reviewers like him could draw attention to Singapore's rich literary output at a time when Singaporeans were unaware of their own literature. Today, twenty years after that conversation, I am happy to report that the literary arts in Singapore are thriving and have both state and community support. There is a growing readership for books by Singapore authors, and a community of internationally recognised novelists and poets whose works have won awards and are included in the school curriculum.

I believe Professor Peter Nazareth is one of the academics who critiques and reviews contributed to this development. His friendship with Singapore writers and poets through the IWP is legendary. The two times he visited Singapore, the poets and writers from Singapore's major languages—Malay, English, Chinese and Tamil writing communities—had hosted him and Mary to lunches and dinners every day. His book, *Edwin Thumboo: Creating a Nation Through Poetry*, which demonstrated his style of literary criticism, has sold out.

In 2009, his chapter on my novel *Fistful Of Colours*, in *Sharing Borders: Studies in Contemporary Singaporean-Malaysian Literature II*, edited by Gwee Li Sui, demonstrated an approach to literary criticism which is very different from the mainstream mode of criticism in which the critic is the sole dominant voice. Peter Nazareth's style is that of 'a communal critic'[1] who is not the sole judge of the writing and who does *not* dominate the critical discourse, but lets the author's voice come through. He invites the reader to participate in the critical discussion, and nudges the reader to assess *Fistful Of Colours* through the dialogue between author and critic. This is a highly interesting and forwarding approach in the age of social media, when many voices prevail. Someday this style will catch on.

Dear Peter,

Wishing you a blessed happy journey toward your 9oth! I wish you more fruitful years of good health and happiness with Mary by your side!

Suchen Christine Lim
Singapore

[1] Saadi Simawe, "Creating a Nation: Peter Nazareth as Literary Critic," a review essay of Peter Nazareth, *Edwin Thumboo: Creating a Nation Through Poetry*, *Asiatic*, vol. 3, no. 1. The Thumboo book was published in the *Interlogue Series*, edited by Kirpal Singh, vol. 7, Ethos Books, 2008.

# THE TIP

Josh Barkan

Peter Nazareth took me to a Chinese restaurant on the Coralville Strip—I assumed he wanted to go there to save money. Or, it wasn't quite just that. I knew it was a favorite place of Peter's, a place he goes to regularly. But for anyone who has grown up in Iowa City, you know the Strip is the place where fast food restaurants, like Long John Silvers and Hardee's can be found, along with a Jiffy Lube car repair shop.

I had grown up in Iowa City, and I used to live about six blocks away from the Strip, in a nice part of town. It was funny how fast you could go from the lawns and ravines of Manville Heights to the Strip. Iowa City is like that—subtle, quick changes.

Peter had made a big point of telling me he wanted to take me out to lunch. He was buying. He was treating. Another reason, I thought, he might want to go someplace not too expensive. I had just visited his class, where he was teaching a novel of mine. Peter is a big fan of Ishmael Reed, and he told me my book was on the syllabus with Reed's. Peter's a good reader, a reader who "gets" what you are writing about, even when what you are writing about is sometimes a bit hidden. He makes the connections, the synapses, like some kind of psychologist reading the subconscious mind of his patient—the author and text. That's why I always enjoyed spending time with Peter. He offered a reflection of oneself, a dive into the hidden interior, and he would come out of the muck with a handful of meaning, of seaweed in his hand, from the bottom of the ocean. I was proud to be on that syllabus, proud to be someplace next to

Reed, next to others Nazareth had decided had merit.

The restaurant on the Strip may have been called the Peking Buffet. When I look on Google Maps, that's the only place that seems to fit where I went with Peter. The name was that nondescript. The Peking Buffet gets a rating of 3.4 stars. The buffet, I remember, was very large. Lots of food, in the way inexpensive places try to give you quantity over quality. The food was fine, nothing bad, nothing that good. I could see why Peter had come to like the place. It was ample and dependable.

But that's not why I'm telling you about this story. It was the tip, I will never forget. The tip that Peter left at the end of the meal. We ate for an hour, talking about writers, Peter weaving in and out stories of Goa, stories about his Elvis course, stories about his youthful days at Makerere. To go out with Peter was to go on a journey of nostalgia, but it wasn't just nostalgia, it was to take you through the difficulties of the past to see a way to go forward, to find strength in the present. Peter was a builder, building hope, building connections between the past and present, creating a coherent thread to his life and to our lives, bobbing and weaving, drawing all things together into one, saying that "this matters" this searching for meaning, this searching to give the voice of empathy in writing, this digging of literature through our personal and cultural entrails.

And then the tip. The bill itself was cheap. $12 for two people for lunch. The waiter, a somewhat older lady who looked tired from working, came over eagerly to Peter. She gave Peter the credit card bill to sign, and Peter left a $12 tip. The total came to $24.

When the waiter was gone—smiling, since she had known what was coming—I asked Peter about the large tip, the doubling of the bill.

"Yes, well I like to do that," Peter said. "I come here once a week, and I do that."

When I pressed him a bit more, I could see that, yes, he did it in part for a little bit of good karma. But that wasn't the point. That wasn't the reason. "You know, it just feels right. It just feels like the right thing to do. So I do it," Peter said.

Peter's car, which we had come in, nothing fancy—the car of an English professor. Peter's office, nothing large. Peter's clothes, always nice, but nothing fancy, perhaps a corduroy jacket that had been worn many times before. It was the giving, the connecting, the generosity in language, the generosity in time spoken together, the generosity in reading that mattered. He was mining the texts, he was giving the gold of his language and understanding back to his students and colleagues.

# THE TIME BESSIE HEAD CHECKED INTO HEARTBREAK HOTEL

Julie Markussen

Twenty-five years ago, I took two courses at the University of Iowa with Peter Nazareth—his insanely popular Elvis as Anthology class and his well-noted African Literature course. In October 1995, he told the African Literature class that author Bessie Head had stayed at his home while she was a student at the University of Iowa. He said that during this stay, she repeatedly requested that he play Elvis's anthem, "Heartbreak Hotel," for her. He mentioned that he told her that Elvis had plenty of amazing songs—not just "Heartbreak Hotel"—but, for some reason, she only wanted to hear that song. When we read Head's novel *Maru* in the class, it became clearer to me why this song may have become so important to her.

I wrote the following essay for Professor Nazareth's African Literature course with him in mind as the sole reader. Over the years, he has graciously cited this essay in a book called *In Search of Elvis* (Westview Press, 1997) and in "Path of Thunder: Meeting Bessie Head" (*Research on African Literatures*, vol. 37, no. 4, Indiana University Press, 2006, pp. 221-229).

***

"Heartbreak Hotel" is a song that seems to parallel the plot of *Maru* as it foreshadows the futures of the main characters: Maru, Margaret Cadmore, Jr., Moleka, and Dikeledi. The final verse and chorus of "Heartbreak Hotel" mirror what should be the ending (or beginning—however one views it) of *Maru.*

An explanation of the composition of "Heartbreak Hotel"

is needed to help illustrate this argument that the form and words of the song foresee the outcome of *Maru.* "Heartbreak Hotel" is a song consisting of five verses and five choruses. Each verse of the song describes some aspect of the hotel: "for broken hearted lovers"; "although it's always crowded"; "the desk clerk is dressed in black." The choruses following each verse are the same except for one major difference: the pronouns Elvis sings. In the first chorus, he croons, "I'll be so lonely I could die." In the next two choruses, he sings, "They're so lonely they could die." In the fourth chorus he sings, "You'll be so lonely you could die," and in the fifth and final chorus, "They'll be so lonely they could die." The use of "I," "they," and "you" can stand for the characters in *Maru.*

First, the "I" in the song must refer to Maru, who is the first person to refer to himself as "I" in the novel when he says, "I'll be going home now" (6). A few lines down, he refers to himself in the first person again. Since Head's novel is titled *Maru,* and he is the first character to whom readers are introduced in the text, it is not unreasonable to compare the "I" of "Heartbreak Hotel" with the character of Maru. (It is also worth noting that both *Maru* and Elvis are kings).

If Maru is the "I" in "Heartbreak Hotel," then Margaret Cadmore, Jr., must be the "you" in the analogy. Interestingly, throughout the whole novel, Margaret is only called by her name by other characters a few times. In fact, when she is referred to by name, it is usually by her full name—Margaret Cadmore, Jr. Only the character of Dikeledi calls her by just her first name, and it happens exactly once in the novel. In the majority of the text, she is called simply "you," as in: "You must learn to live with your appearance" (18) and "You will help your people" (17). The children also refer to her as "you" when they say, "You are a bushman" (17). This fact makes it easier to refer to the "you" in "Heartbreak Hotel" as Margaret, Jr. Furthermore, Margaret, Jr. is adopted, so she was given her name by someone outside of her own bloodline. By calling her "you," Head sets her apart as an outsider, as it is a refusal to name her. However, it also allows her to be a universal figure, as Margaret Sr. wants her to be seen. Part of Margaret Sr.'s vision is that she wanted to create an identity for Margaret Jr. that would not fit into any narrow definitions.

The "they" from "Heartbreak Hotel" most readily symbolizes people outside of the main characters of the novel—especially the ones at constant odds with Margaret Jr. For example, the children who make fun of Margaret Jr. are referred to only as "they." One powerful and memorable passage shows children whose parents teach them how to hate. The passage reads:

> "They spat on you. They pinched you. They danced a wild jiggle, with the tin cans rattling: 'Bushman! Low Breed! Bastard!'" (10-11)

Margaret Cadmore Sr. tells Margaret Jr. that the only things that will ever be truly her own are her mind and her soul. This implies her body will never be her own because it will be used by the "theys" in order to have someone upon whom to look down. Margaret Sr. tells Margaret Jr.:

> "They are wrong. You will have to live with your appearance for the rest of your life.
> There is nothing you can do to change it." (18)

Margaret Jr. is forced to build her internal kingdom, or room of the mind and the soul, to compensate for the lack of identity she has through her body.

As discussed in Professor Nazareth's class, like "Heartbreak Hotel," *Maru* deals with the issue of rooms. Presley sings: "Although it's always crowded/You still can find some room." *Maru* is a novel full of crowded rooms, but there is always a way to make more rooms, as discussed in the novel's beginning. There are two literal rooms mentioned by the narrator: the room in which Margaret Jr. loves Maru, and the room in which she loves Moleka. Here, Margaret Jr.'s mind and soul appear to serve as rooms in which she will harbor all of her life experiences, since her own body will belong to society and not to herself. Maru and Moleka, for that matter, also represent the two rooms of the mind and soul—she loves them both and is able to store her life experiences in ways that belong to her. She cannot exist as a whole being without these two "rooms," as they make up her mind and soul, thus creating a paradox of Margaret Sr.'s idea that her mind and soul will be the only things that truly belong to Margaret Jr. In truth, her mind and soul are made up of bits and pieces of her environment—such as Maru and Moleka, but she, as a separate person, cannot exist wholly without them. Maru and Moleka further stand for the mind and the soul when Moleka says to Margaret Jr., upon taking the room: "You see, you don't have to be afraid anymore. First there was one of you. Now there are two of you" (31). When she takes the room at Moleka's, she is actually opening up a room for either her mind or soul to enter—the other room is later filled by Moleka.

Finally, "Heartbreak Hotel" becomes the ultimate metaphor for the outcome of the characters of *Maru*. Since the chorus pronouns progress in a pattern in "Heartbreak Hotel" as "I," "they," "they," "you," and "they," this indicates the outcome of *Maru*, the cruel people of society, and Margaret Jr. When Maru and Margaret Jr. marry and move away, the narrator suggests that the people kept their prejudices and pretended that Maru died. In "Heartbreak Hotel," there is an instance where all the characters are together at the hotel—all in loneliness: Maru (I), the people (they), and Margaret (you). This exists until the musical interlude sets up the change. The musical break gives way for an escape for the "I" (Maru) and "you" (Margaret Jr.), and in the end and final chorus, the only people that emerge as lonely are the "theys." I see the "I" and "you" as separate from the "they"; otherwise, it would be logical that Presley would sing "We'll be so lonely we could die." But the "you" and "I" are separated, which implies that in the end, Maru and Margaret will emerge from the loneliness of "Heartbreak Hotel," while the people of the cruel society will remain on Lonely Street. Readers can only hope that Maru and Margaret make it to Hotel Happiness.

***

In his notes to me on the final graded essay, Professor Nazareth mentioned that there are still other "rooms" yet to be explored in *Maru*—especially the way the "room" opens for the Marsarwa people at the end of the novel. I wish to thank Peter Nazareth for his wisdom, guidance, feedback, passion, and inspiration over the years. What I learned all those years ago is still an enduring part of my education, and I sincerely owe that to him.

## WORKS CITED

Head, Bessie. *Maru*. Heinemann, 1971.
Presley, Elvis. "Heartbreak Hotel." RCA, 1956.

# ALL I HAVE TO DO IS DREAM

Rochelle Nameroff

The first chord hits and sort of wavers there, sounding slightly underwater for a moment, gauzy, transparent, seeming to disappear and echo at the same time. Then two soft tenor voices emerge from this odd sensation of imbalance, this suspension between delicacy and warp, the voices in a harmony so right you're not sure if it's one person or two.

These are the Everly Brothers, and their satisfying blend has been a mystery and a joy to me from their first entry into the fog of my adolescence to right now, curled up in my basement apartment with the grooved black platter going round on my old Sears turntable.

It isn't the long-playing records that I remember but small thick 45s, a huge hole gone in the middle, familiar-circles you could one-hand onto the thick plug of the record player. A big stack of 45s like metal pancakes, each one making a thud as it dropped. I miss that dropping sound. It set up a rhythm of anticipation and separation that is missing on long-playing records. After I've played an LP more than twice I usually know what's going to happen, and each song will later carry the memory, the foreknowledge of the one next in line, a ghost memory that has no surprise in it.

One of my friends says the Everlys are best heard in cars, coasting down a highway in an old Chevrolet, windows open, one hand in-between the whoosh of air and the heat of the chrome, a stutter of static on the radio. Another friend luxuriates in the memory of slow dancing in basement rec rooms, the nuzzle of bodies somehow part of the song.

I remember all this, and more. I'll never turn down a hug or a dance, and the intermixture is like some pure exalted permission, but what I remember most is the singing along, the harmonizing. Walking down Hadley or Center Street all the way to school, singing with Sandy and Sonia who lived down the block. They were twins. Sandy and Sonia, though one was skinny and one wasn't. One wore glasses and the other had clear unblemished sight. They were nothing like each other. They didn't even get along.

We sang "Heart of My Heart," "Sentimental Journey" (our parents' standards), "You Belong to Me" by Patience and Prudence, and mostly the songs of the Everly Brothers. We were in Choir together, my favorite class, but we didn't sing choir songs on the way to school. I used to love Choir so much that my mother, seeing her Jewish daughter transfixed while singing Christmas carols, would yank me out yearly, relenting only after a plea from Mr. Goodrich, the avuncular choir director. No Svengali, Mr. Goodrich. What my mother didn't understand was that the words could have been anything, that I was already following another religion altogether.

Singing in harmony—little gives me such complete satisfaction. When it works, even when it doesn't, there must be some kind of dream in the meshing of notes.

And nobody could dream this like the Everly Brothers. We weren't always sure which was which, or who had the highest pompadour, who was the youngest or the cutest (I think it was Phil), but there was no sound quite like theirs. Some of the lyrics were funny, and even silly-naive and stilted like a lot of country music. Somehow this made something even sweeter. In "Wake Up, Little Susie" they worry:

*We both went sound asleep.*

*Wake up, uh, Little Susie and weep.*
*The movie's over, it's 4:00,*
*And we're in trouble deep.*

And there were other adolescent complaints ("He's a bird dog!") and problems ("Problems, problems, problems all day long") like a lot of rock and roll. But it was the harmony they sang that transformed and transfigured their music.

The Everly Brothers grew up in a singing family; Margaret and Ike Everly (Mom and Pop) were professional country and western musicians in the South and Midwest. They had a radio show on KMA in Shenandoah, Iowa, where Don and Phil, then eight and six years old, first sang publicly in 1945. They sang with the family act until the parents retired in the 1950s and the boys graduated from high school. There are many family singing groups, and all show some intuitive vocal knowledge of the others, their nuances, shadings and progressions. If you sing with other people, you come to anticipate their sounds like you know the language of your friends. Or not the language—that's too large a concept—but perhaps a kind of shorthand, an emotional grammar.

It's odd how we know a voice, and what that voice, no matter the distance of years, can recall to the ear. An old lover phoned the other night, and I listened, breath almost held—Pound says the Chinese ideogram for red contains the condensed pictures for "rose," "iron rust," "cherry," and "flamingo." If I could take a voiceprint, would it print out the details like an ideogram? The slanted, tiny search I hear in his not-exactly tenor, the syncopation of pause and slight burr that tells me something funny will follow, the lowered sad notes. How one's name is said.

I once had a boyfriend from Texas who always called me

Rochelle instead of my nickname. Actually, he wasn't originally from Texas but had adopted it as his emotional home so he drawled better than any good ol' boy. He would say, "Ro-celle. Go get your um-brella," accenting and prolonging both first syllables as if the words were part of a song and talking a form of music. But he was always at a distance, and I even think of his voice as a story. Some voices come closer than that, seeming almost to live inside as well as outside, as when you hear yourself in the sudden intonation of your parents, those vocal gestures you thought so far away, those bodies.

The Everly Brothers seem to me to sound closer than lover or parent, submerged in each other, two halves of not one voice but not quite two, as if the divided (but not opposed) self could be externalized, doubled but not twinned, one a ghost-step ahead, the other separate but entwined. It feels like a stage of not quite differentiation, sort of an amphibian crawling onto the next embryonic land. It feels like the blurring of inside and outside, which is desirable and unearthly, and I think it is this unearthly knowledge of the other that gives the Everlys such perfect harmony.

It is not the self. It is not narcissism. There is something missing in each voice alone. Even with a tape, the self cannot really harmonize with itself just as the mouth cannot know its own kiss. The sound of the Everlys gets closer, giving a promise of harmony in division, but a love without opposition. This sounds like psychology, but I want it to describe the soul.

Of course, in teenage music there is so much that is a blur of hormones and dream that all these terms may be silly. It is not like the hurt animal sound of Hank Williams or the lovesick abandonment of Judy Garland—grownup torch sounds that are as unbearable as they are exquisite. That kind of longing has an unfillable mouth, a knowledge of absence that is tattoo-like.

The closest the Everlys come to this is a type of yodel, but in harmony. The yodel itself is a solitary form, and if you listen to the yodel of Hank Williams you'll hear a sound almost animal. Yodeling developed perhaps as a solitary dialogue, hearing sound echo off the landscape, call and recall, but maybe just a community of one. However, there is something unusual in the knowledge of that "one." The shift of gears into the falsetto is so exciting and so sexual as the voice slides over some invisible membrane, a listener, if there is one, cannot help but respond. When that slide happens, something wonderful escapes, and there is a transformation—or is it a merging—of male into female, pain into joy.

*And when I leave,*
*I'll be a long time gone.*

On the word "leave," the perfect word to stretch into another realm of expression, the Everlys shift into this special gear, this place of sound that seems to know something, this—religion might call it—leap of faith to somewhere else.

I don't plan to write about that place. Gospel music sings about crossing the river, and the myths of many cultures intuit some watery journey. Birth or death, sexual passion or crying—if the music claims knowledge of that journey, the harmony is a wish that we don't go alone.

Of course the Everly (I almost wrote Every) Brothers, as I knew them, broke up. Conflict, individual egos, marriages, money, drugs, alcohol—a normal ideogram of life in the late twentieth century. The pressures of being a duo, a Brother, or just a member of a group are familiar stories. Like Simon and Garfunkel, another blend that once wished to bridge the troubled waters, the Everlys ended their twenty-eight-year partnership, and for ten years didn't even speak to each other. When the Beatles broke up, journalists and essayists mourned that "the dream was over." What does music dream for a culture?

*The only trouble is*
*Gee whiz*
*I'm dreaming my life away.*

Yes, I know. The Brothers are back together again, and the critics praise the grown-up depth and richness, the new echoes in their harmony, as if only through conflict can one express a true love. And yes, I agree they sound wonderful, a full trombone, and if I hear something missing I am probably listening for my lost adolescence, the sudden surprise of a new song, the unknown body across the dance floor, the personal town. I know what song is next on the turntable.

Perhaps they're right. I know I'm supposed to agree and call my dream "nostalgia," tucking it into its proper place, a sort of miniature, patting my old self with sweet condescension. Nice old self. Foolish nice old self.

## GOLD FROM UGANDA

*For Peter Nazareth, with gratitude*

His is a pioneering spirit
For he wrote the nation into modernity
And produced stunning work
Challenging sectarianism
And declaring the brown hue
An East African reality.

His is a hawk eye
That saw black bigots for who they were –
Destroyers of the country
And enemies of all people
Black, brown, or blue.

His is a pan-human vision
For he embraces every person
Irrespective of colour, creed, or class
And connects the south with the north
The east with the west

His is a celestial heart
For he breathes life into humans
Firing them off
To lofty heights of victory
Never imagined before

His is a life that shines far and wide
Illuminating the dark corners of humanity
And communicating an important truth –

It is possible to rise above racial pettiness
And make the world a better home for all.

Danson Kahyana

# ROUTES AND ROOTS: NARRATING BLACK LIBERATORY CONSCIOUSNESS IN *WIZARD OF THE CROW*

Raquel Baker

> I've never written that book that I really wanted to write. You can argue that every novel I've written is an attempt to write that novel. I want to write that novel that really, really empowers people.
> –Ngũgĩ wa Thiong'o
> (qtd. by Sulaiman)

> In the spirit of the dead, the living, and the unborn,
> Empty your ears of all impurities, o listener,
> That you may hear my story
> –Ngũgĩ wa Thiong'o
> *Wizard of the Crow* (Dedication)

If, as Indigenous knowledges tell us, a profound aspect of what we are is story, then transformation to more critical modes of consciousness will require new forms of narration. If what we are is story, then transforming contemporary geopolitical dynamics to achieve will require new ways to narrate our selves. In the speculative novel *Wizard of the Crow* (2006), Kenyan novelist Ngũgĩ wa Thiong'o works on narrative space by casting it as a "performative space, a contested political space [of] reflection and action" where the transformation of African postcoloniality can be imagined (Lovesey 140). Ngũgĩ mediates this regeneration, or re-visioning, of African postcoloniality through the narration of the fictitious Free Republic of Aburĩria and the relationship between its people, its ruling elite, and its ruler. In an interview for *Kirkus Review*, Ngũgĩ explains the figure of the president of Aburĩria, known in the novel only as "the Ruler"; he states, "I was inspired by Mobutu in Zaire, Amin in Uganda, Bokassa in Central Africa, Suharto in Indonesia, Pinochet in Chile—all dictators who were sponsored by the West and were *account*-able to no one" (my emphasis 16). And let us not forget Marcos in the Philippines, Biya in Cameroon, Vorster in South Africa, Mugabe in Zimbabwe, or Trump working in the heart of the West itself. As an assemblage of historical leaders, the ruler of Aburĩria invokes the power of post-independence statecraft: excessive, cruel, dependent on transnational capital, and accountable to no one. Through the pure absurdity of this character's regime, the novel's narration stages a meditation on *account*ability in all of its senses: the account as but one version of the story; the account as a call to responsibility; and the account as a way to tell, to mark, to memorialize—as a way to remember what the hopes for independence were: to realize decolonization as mode of anti-colonial consciousness—as a more inclusive, expansive ode of belonging—rather than simply as a form of governmentality that transfers power from colonial regimes to native elites. In other words, the authoritative narration critiques decolonization achieved through governance in order to assert decolonization as a form of oppositional consciousness, where decolonization becomes a mode of subjectivity than binds the individual to the collective rather than a mode of sovereignty that incorporates an individual into a body politic.

Such a desire for decolonization goes beyond positing the creation of a Black-ruled nation as the ultimate measure of liberation and points towards Frantz Fanon's seminal formulation in *The Wretched of the Earth*, where the concept of decolonization is defined as "a complete calling in question of the colonial situation" that "influences individuals and modifies them fundamentally" (37, 36). Fanon's project of decolonization goes beyond the construction of a nation and into the construction of a decolonized subject by embracing "decolonization [as] the veritable creation of a new man" (36). Following Fanon, postcolonial theorist Homi Bhabha also defines decolonization in this deeper sense as "a plan of action as well as a projected aspiration" (in Fanon xvi, xvii). Here, the temporal aspect of decolonization is emphasized by defining it as a mode of desire—an aspiration for the future that informs processes of identification, consciousness, and the experience of self and other. The major themes of Ngũgĩ's novel—the liberatory realizations of individual and collective power—both reflect and rework Fanon's conception of decolonization. The novel's critique of reactionary forms of African independence privileges the conception of decolonization as the creation of the new—new forms of consciousness, identification, and non-binary subject positions; more expansive notions of Blackness; and new forms of belonging, particularly beyond national and racial imaginaries. In relation to Fanon's formulation of decolonization, Ngũgĩ represents decolonization not simply as the creation of a new man but rather as the creation of a new oppositional consciousness that affirms gender synergy and an expansive, diasporic Black consciousness. Such a narrative of decolonization writes against hierarchical gender relations, the universal rhetoric of *man* for *human*, or Blackness that is parsed into national belongings. As such, Ngũgĩ's work can be read productively as a positioning of story and narration as sites of decolonizing work.

As a work of speculative fiction, Ngũgĩ's novel suggests that it is the African imaginary itself that is in need of decolonization.

By the imaginary, I refer to the complex of desires, images, stereotypes, expectations, models, ideas, dreams, nightmares, beliefs, anxieties, representations, narratives, metaphors, interpretations, and memories that inform our construction of reality—our sense of ourselves and of the world around us. Historian Ann Stoler theorizes that targeting the intimate sphere and internal space of colonial subjects is as important to colonial power as the external imposition of expropriating land due to the ways in which "intimate domains . . . figure in the making of racial categories and in the management of imperial rule" (829). This colonization of internal space comprises what historian Geoff Eley calls "the colonial effect":

> We might think of this "colonial effect" as the sum of the transference and translation of meanings made far away from European homelands during the relentless drives of European expansionism. Such meanings were based in an entire complex of perceptions and encounters, including disorderly and heterogeneous knowledge; idioms of thought; direct and vicarious experiences; spectacular events; arresting and seductive images; compelling arguments about economics, prosperity, and global survival; a visual repertoire of fantasy and desire; manifold forms of everyday consumption; and all the relevant registers of government action. Over time, that aggregative, malleable, and extraordinarily ramified discursive presence could acquire an interpellative coerence that we have come to call, in summary form, colonialism. (19)

Given colonialism's ability to constitute discourses that inform knowledge of self and other, the decolonization of discursive space becomes as important to the production of oppositional consciousness as re-asserting sovereignty over external space. Contemporary theory in academic disciplines from history to anthropology postulate colonialism's profound effect on subjectivity; these internalized effects constitute the primary psychic problematic of decolonization, moving the focus from how to take back land to how to take back self. Within this internal focus, the primary illness that decolonization must address is one of identity, both individual and collective.

In *Decolonising the Mind* (1986), Ngũgĩ writes that "the prescription of the correct cure is dependent on a rigorous analysis of the reality" (xi). Here again, Ngũgĩ brings us to the realization that the discourses through which we construct reality are fundamental to constructing a cure. Given this frame, Ngũgĩ argues that the two key issues relevant to understanding African reality, as well as Africa's destiny as a whole, are imperialism and the question of language. Ngũgĩ defines imperialism as "the rule of consolidated finance capital," and he further notes that "it has economic, political, military, cultural and psychological consequences for the people of the world today" (*Decolonising the Mind* 2). Ngũgĩ's focus on imperialism connects the contemporary African context to larger global institutions. He writes,

> The present predicaments of Africa are often not a matter of personal choice: they arise from an historical situation. Their solutions are not so much a matter of personal choice as that of a fundamental social transformation of the structures of our societies starting with a real break with imperialism and its internal ruling allies. Imperialism and its comprador alliances in Africa can never develop the continent. ... The imperialist tradition

> in Africa today is maintained by the international bourgeoisie using the multinational and of course the flag-waving ruling classes. The economic and political dependence of this African neo-liberal bourgeoisie is reflected in its culture of apemanship and parrotry enforced on a restive population through police boots, barbed wire, a gowned clergy and judiciary. (*Decolonising the Mind* xii, 2)

For Ngũgĩ, stereotypical knowledge about Africa is produced in order to disavow the need for the real structural changes that would be necessary to ameliorate the fundamental inequities facing Africa today. He writes, "The misleading stock interpretation of the African realities has been popularized by the western media which likes to deflect people from seeing that imperialism is still the root cause of many problems in Africa. Unfortunately, some African intellectuals have fallen victims … to that scheme" (*Decolonising the Mind* 1). Ngũgĩ's primary claim in *Decolonising the Mind* is the issue taken up by contemporary discourses on empire: the devastating subjective effects of imperialism. Ngũgĩ writes,

> [T]he biggest weapon wielded and actually daily unleashed by imperialism against that collective defiance is the cultural bomb. The effect of the cultural bomb is to annihilate a people's belief in their names, in their languages, in their environment, in their heritage of struggle, in their unity, in their capacities and ultimately in themselves. It makes them see their past as one wasteland of non-achievement and it makes them want to distance themselves from that wasteland. It makes them want to identify with that which is furthest removed

> from themselves; for instance, with other peoples' languages rather than their own. (3)

The crippling effects of this cultural bomb give rise to the centrality of the question of language in relation to decolonization and resistance. Ngũgĩ addresses this issue by making a commitment to the practice of writing in African languages in order to enrich African cultural production because, for Ngũgĩ, language is a product of collective history that helps to construct and understand the present. In "A Statement" in *Decolonising the Mind*, Ngũgĩ writes, "This book, *Decolonising the Mind*, is my farewell to English as a vehicle for any of my writings. From now on it is Gĩkũyũ and Kiswahili all the way" (xiv). In an interview with Michael Pozo, Ngũgĩ modifies this statement to say that "while in [prison], I thought a great deal about the relationship between English, as the imperial language, and now the language of power in a postcolonial state, and African languages, and I took the irrevocable position never to write my *fiction and drama* in English again" (my emphasis). *Wizard of the Crow* bears witness to this oath; the novel was written in Gĩkũyũ and translated into English by the author. Ngũgĩ's theoretical work, such as *Something Torn and New: An African Renaissance* (2009), is written in English. The distinction between his theoretical and literary work emphasizes the audience each text is written for, as well as the import of the power of aesthetic, or literary work to constitute communal and individual modes of identification. Ngũgĩ's commitment to producing literary work in his mother tongue positions decolonization as the critical project of transforming social, political, intellectual, and cultural structures, including the values that are perpetuated through modes of representation.

## THE LITERARY AS THE SPACE TO MAKE MANIFEST

> Style is a performative, epistemological act.
> –Martha Nussbaum
> *Love's Knowledge* (3)

> The destroyed ... retain the desire to remake themselves and act upon that desire to remake themselves. The remade are pointers to the way, the way of remembrance, the way of knowing purpose.
> –Ayi Kwei Armah
> *Two Thousand Seasons* (xvii)

In relation to decolonization—in relation to the creation of the new—style matters. *Wizard of the Crow* works as a site of decolonization through the way that it positions the reader to question how Africa is represented for itself and for the world. The novel positions the reader in this way through its style. The satirical style uses the circuits of pleasure—the hilariously funny scenes—to seduce the reader into engaging with Ngũgĩ's insightful commentary about the absurdity of global ruling elites, both in Aburĩria/Africa and in the West/U.S. Ngũgĩ's hard-hitting satire positions his reader to critique power and to apprehend the urgency of the need to reclaim and transform cultural, political, and economic institutions. Language is critical to this project. In relation to the issue of language, this novel is positioned as a site of decolonization because of its language of production and its system of allusions. Most important, the novel was written in Gĩkũyũ. For Ngũgĩ, writing in Gĩkũyũ is "an act of literary and political intervention" (*Decolonising the Mind* xi). Ngũgĩ translated the novel into English to make its wisdom available in a wider dialogue, which is particularly important for Africans in the diaspora. But by writing the book in Gĩkũyũ, Ngũgĩ is contributing to the cultural development and memory of the Kikuyu peoples—enriching the African imaginary in a culturally specific manner. This act bears witness to the development of the argument in Ngũgĩ's critical work that the reconstruction most crucial to African decolonization is that of self-image—what Ngũgĩ calls the "re-membering of Africa" (*Something Torn and New: An African Renaissance* ix). For Ngũgĩ, "language, culture, and social memory" are crucial to this project (*Something Torn and New* x).

In addition to its language of production, one of the central allusions of the novel also relates to the issue of language. One of the storylines that moves the plot forward is the Heavenscrape project, referred to as Marching to Heaven, a "Modern House of Babel" (Ngũgĩ, *Wizard* 17) that would extend "to the gates of Heaven so that the Ruler could call on God daily to say good morning or good evening or simply how was your day today, God? The Ruler would be the daily recipient of God's advice, resulting in the rapid growth of Aburĩria to heights never dreamt by humans" (16). Here we can see the satirical ironic distance of the narration, creating a tone that makes us laugh at the spectacle of modernity even as the absurdity of the project allows us to also question the engine of what Ngũgĩ calls "capitalist modernity" (*Something Torn and New* 5).

Capitalist modernity refers to a world-systems analysis of social reality. From this perspective, the current modern world-system is a capitalist market economy that began in the sixteenth century. Capitalism requires expansion; this expansion extends not only into markets but also into the very imaginaries of modernity by defining the conditions of possibility that structure knowledge (Wallerstein). For Africa, this expansion was the engine of colonialism. For Ngũgĩ, colonialism is "simultaneously the foundation, fuel, and consequence of Europe's capitalist modernity" (*Something Torn and New* 5). For this reason, Ngũgĩ asserts that what is at stake in the liberatory project is "the decolonization of modernity itself" (*Something Torn and New* xi).

Ngũgĩ makes the claim that a primary consequence of global capitalist expansion through its engine of colonialism was the dismemberment of Africa "into two halves: the continent and its diaspora" (*Something Torn and New* 5). Ngũgĩ invokes the salience of this issue through the thematic resonance of the Marching to Heaven project, which calls upon the archetypal mythology of the Tower of Babel. In Christian mythology, the Tower of Babel was built by the Babylonians to reach up to heaven not to praise God but instead to make a name for themselves. God's punishment for such hubris was the dismemberment of humanity's unity: the division of the earth's one language into many, and the scattering of the peoples throughout the globe. Similar stories exist in the Judaic, Islamic, Central American, South Asian, and African traditions. By invoking this narrative, Ngũgĩ puts the themes of the origins of nations and languages and the folly of humanity's arrogance, decadence, and diaspora into play. The themes of decadence, diaspora, and language are particularly important to *Wizard of the Crow.* The novel's focus on language privileges the issue of representation. Focusing on the issue of representation foregrounds the importance of narration and narrative style. Ngũgĩ uses satire to cohere the elements of his primary representational strategy, which is to combine speculative devices with attitudes and values of postcolonial resistance and re-memberance. Ngũgĩ uses speculative devices to create a mixture of realistic and absurd elements that harness the revelatory power of satire to re-member Black liberatory identification in the face of postcolonial dismemberment. His representational strategies use imagination, rather than logic, as a mode of transformation and decolonization, as way to reroute speculation—a key mode of desire and future-oriented aspiration in capitalism—into liberatory projection. As modes of thinking, both imagination and logic are representational systems; as such, both use symbolic techniques to establish perceptions—to allow users to become aware of things. Ngũgĩ's imaginative mode privileges hyperbole and burlesque over the scientific method and reason, key privileged aspects of Western Enlightenment modernity, which Ngũgĩ critiques by poking fun at the cultish faith invested in logic and "a Frenchman named Descartes" (378). It is not only the conceit of the Tower of Babel that organizes the primary themes of the novel but also the very form of the novel itself as a literary work—"a reworking of reality into a symbolic narration"—that allows the novel to foreground questions of representation (Wildenthal 188). This novel narrates liberatory Black identification through a series of imaginative representtations—transformations, exaggerations, literalizations, oppositions, conceits, and satirical moments. Moreover, the narrative of the development of, or path to, such an expansive Black identification is not represented as a singular, coherent entity, but rather as a complex set of simultaneously interacting, countervailing, and competing stories, songs, dances, knowledges, and memories. In this way, the narrative and narration of decolonization is represented as performative, improvisational, theatrical—as an embodied imaginative practice.

The novel serves as a site of decolonization through the way in which its formal structure constantly positions the reader to apprehend, re-vision, and question the physical, moral, and intellectual absurdities of imperialism, authoritarian corruption, and despotism. In Book One of the novel, "Power Daemons," Ngũgĩ's trenchant, satirical narration represents the uneven relations of power between Africa and the West, which are maintained not only by neo-colonial economic relations but also by the reservoir of stereotypical images in the postcolonial imaginary. Ngũgĩ represents both issues through the stark oppositions, absurdities, and outrages called out in his narration. Describing the scene outside of a luxury hotel frequented by tourists, beggars, and prostitutes alike, Ngũgĩ writes,

> Sometimes the police raided the beggars, but just for show, for Aburĩria's prisons were already full. Most beggars would have been quite happy to be jailed for the meal and a bed. The government also had to be mindful not to upset tourism by sweeping too many beggars off the streets. Pictures of beggars or wild animals were what many tourists sent back as proof of having been in Africa. In Aburĩria, wild animals were becoming rare because of dwindling forests and poaching, and tourist pictures of beggars or children with kwashiorkor and flies massing around their runny noses and sore eyes were prized for authenticity. If there were no beggars in the streets, tourists might start doubting whether Aburĩria was an authentic African country. (35)

Here Ngũgĩ astutely pinpoints the way that Africa's difference—its enforced economic inferiority in relation to the West—becomes its greatest commodity. Stereotypical images of decadence become Africa's mark of authenticity. These prized tourist images support two key myths in the Western imaginary: "*(1) the myth of progress and (2) the myth of white, Western superiority*" (Dinerstein 572). Through the absurd and acerbic afflictions of his characters, Ngũgĩ also illustrates how these two myths are as important in the imaginary of African elites as they are in the Western imaginary.

## WHITENESS IN THE AFRICAN IMAGINARY

> Racial representation is central to the organization of the modern world.
> –Richard Dyer
> (*White: Essays on Race and Culture* 1)

Ngũgĩ engages with this problem of the African imaginary through his main trope of sickness. Through the trope of sickness whiteness is positioned as part of the construction of the African self—as part of the lens through which some modes of African subjectivity are constituted. Because this constitution is also a concomitant devaluing and negation of Blackness, the way in which whiteness constitutes modes of self-identification and is embedded in social practices is debilitatingly monstrous. In addition to the Ruler's "mysterious illness that defied all logic and medical expertise" introduced in Book One, in Book Two, "Queuing Daemons," Ngũgĩ inflicts an elite businessman, Tarjirika, with the "If only" disease; all he can say is "If! If only" (4, 143). Twelve chapters after its introduction, Ngũgĩ reveals Tarjirika's true affliction: white-ache. Tarjirika stammers, "If . . . My . . . Skin . . . Were not . . . Black. . . . If only . . . My skin . . . Were . . . white . . . like a . . . white man's . . . skin. . . . Oh, if only my skin were white!" (179). Here, humor works not to express the inexorable colonization of African desire; instead, it is used to reveal the salience of white supremacy in the African imaginary. By literalizing internalized colonial values as the psychosis of white-ache, Ngũgĩ exposes the irretrievable absurdity of the Eurocentric cultural order that creates such a condition. Here colonial values not only refer to economic and political structures but also to symbolic economies that constitute color hierarchies and relate colors to meaning, worth, and worthiness. As a conceit, the disease of white-ache suggests not a double consciousness, as in Dubois's generative theory, but a fundamentally self-negating consciousness. Ngũgĩ uses humor as a tactic to make manifest the realities of postcolonial identification and the politics of skin color. Externalizing the ridiculous effects of racist postcolonial symbolic systems and the hierarchical capitalist order that they undergird serves as a mode of resistance to the authority of such a socio-political order.

Given the specific imperial and colonial histories that hastened Africa's uneven integration into the global capitalist market economy, whiteness has materialized as a powerful trope for success, progress, and possibility. In response, Ngũgĩ's strategy is to materialize and make manifest the continuing social and political realities of such uneven integration, from messianic neo-colonial rule to the deeply racialized discourses that inform postcolonial national and personal modes of identification. Within these discourses, progress is equated to the accumulation of wealth; civilization is equated to social position; and, through a metonymic slippage on the level of cultural representation, whiteness comes to stand in for them all. Due to this slippage, the disparate experience of Africa in relation to the West is read as black barbarity and biological inferiority. Within such a symbolic order, issues of *class* and political hierarchy, such as ruling-class elite *domination,* are represented and internalized as *racial* issues. Given this articulation of representational systems to processes of identification, Tarjirika's If Only disease perfectly foregrounds the relation of self-consciousness to issues of language. The disease represents yearning explicitly as both an interrupted utterance—a stoppage, an interruption of language—and a racial barrier. Through the trope of white-ache, Ngũgĩ represents the effects of race as a social obstruction by literally rendering it as an obstruction of language. Through this figural turn, the disease of white-ache exposes the metonymic slippage that turns *geo-political economic* relations that determine the allocation of power, prestige, and wealth into *racial* experiences. The disease of white-ache clearly illustrates the symbolic economies that are produced as effects of material economies. Through this figural rendering of white-ache as a literal disease, Ngũgĩ articulates a central tenet of contemporary theories of subjectivity: material practices constitute subject positions. But unlike theoretical texts, Ngũgĩ's literary style articulates the concept concretely—clearly, in such a way that the reader can get hold of the concept and not only see it but also see it as absurd and self-abhorrent rather than as a naturalized truth. This move underscores one of the primary representational strategies used in the novel: to render life-disavowing socio-political practices literally as stoppages, breaks, and frozen moments.

Through this strategy, Ngũgĩ uses narrative space to literalize the temporal effects of discourses of national sovereignty. In a poignant scene in Book One, the Ruler's wife, Rachael, asks him to stop having affairs with schoolgirls. She chides him, "Have you not tears of concern for our tomorrow" (6)? The Ruler lashes out at his wife with impunity, wanting "to make Rachael understand that he, the Ruler, has power, real power over everything including . . . yes . . . Time" (7). The Ruler banishes his wife to a mansion "to give her time to think" (7). Ngũgĩ brilliantly elaborates on Rachael's predicament to draw out the devastating temporal effects of discourses of national sovereignty:

> All the clocks in the house were frozen at the second, the minute, and the hour that she had raised the question of schoolgirls; the calendars pointed to the day and the

> year. The clocks tick-tocked but their hands did not move. The mechanical calendar always flipped to the same date. The food provided was the same as at the last supper, the clothes the same as she had worn that night. The bedding and curtains were identical to those where she had once lived. The television and radio kept repeating programs that were on during the last supper. Everything in the new mansion reproduced the exact moment.
>
> A record player was programmed to play only one hymn:
>
> *Our Lord will come back one day*
> *He will take us to his home above*
> *I will then know how much he loves me*
> *Whenever he comes back*
>
> Rachael would remain thus, awaiting his second coming, and on that day when he found that she had shed all the tears for all the tomorrows of all the children she had accused him of abusing, he would take her back to restart life exactly from where it had stopped, or rather Rachael would resume her life, which had been marking time, like a cinematic frame on pause. I am your beginning and your end.
>
> What were you before I made you my wife? … I am the past and the present you have been and *I am your tomorrow take it or leave it*, he added in English as he turned his back on her. (8-9)

As with the Tower of Babel allusion, here Ngũgĩ also reworks biblical stories in the context of African postcoloniality. In addition, as with the play on the Tower of Babel, invoking the biblical Rachel also carries the thematic resonance of diaspora.

But unlike the biblical Rachel, who shed tears for the exiled Jews, Ngũgĩ's Rachael refuses to shed tears for the Ruler; she refuses to give him what he wants: "her self-abnegation" (10). In opposition to Tarjirika, Rachael is strong-willed—a figure of opposition. This image represents, literalizes, the frozen present that despotism gives rise to. As with the Ruler's relationship with Rachael, all despotic relations—whether between individuals, a people and their government, nations, or nations and institutions—have the same effect: to dispossess in the present and hold hostage the future.

The aesthetics of *Wizard of the Crow* are structured around literalizing the absurdity of the despotic relations of neo-colonialism that define contemporary postcoloniality, whether these be national, transnational, interpersonal, or intimate relations. The overall effect of the exaggerated situations and images in the novel is to make real, to literalize, the effects of imperialism and neo-colonialism; and, ultimately, to reveal "the vitality, strength and beauty of resistance" (*Decolonising the Mind* ix). In addition to using satire deconstructively to reveal the absurdity of neo-colonial relations, the novel also uses satire constructively to decolonize the African imaginary. The novel's symbolic economy troubles stereotypical images of Africa by putting multiplicity and difference into play. The novel's central conceit is the circulation of multiple stories about what caused the Ruler's illness. The central trope of the circulation of multiple versions of the story is a way to critique the concentration of power that Ngũgĩ satirically pokes fun at throughout the novel, one clever instance being the reference to a book titled *People Make History, Then A Ruler Makes It His Story* (20). Relating multiplicity to the concept of history foregrounds the impossibility of getting to one truth and, therefore, critiques official historical narratives, which Ngũgĩ also suggests are remade in the name of elite power.

Multiplicity is also at work in the novel's character development. The novel's central protagonist is not a single character, but two characters, each with multiple identities. As a unit, the male protagonist Kamĩtĩ and female protagonist Nyawĩra serve to foreground the necessity of gender synergy, underscoring the necessity for a critical analysis of gender in imaginaries of decolonization. Nyawĩra herself has multiple versions of her name:

> At Brilliant Girls High School, Nyawĩra went through a period when she really struggled with her names. There was a time when she called herself Engenethi Nyawĩra Charles Matthew Mũgwanja Wangahũ, often writing it as E.N.C.M.M. Wangahũ. She was not very keen on Engenethi and became Grace Mũgwanja. Grace Mũgwanja stuck, mostly in the village community, and … to her parents she would always be either Engenethi or Grace. She herself continued struggling with these markers of identity. (78)

Here we see her names changing, representing her differently to different communities, and ultimately functioning as markers of her identity. In this way, Nyawĩra's name suggests how multiplicity, transformation, and representation are intimately tied to subjectivity and identification. In addition, the mix of female and male names underscores a gender politics that binds men and women together, working against hierarchical, patriarchal social orders and modes of identification.

The primary figure that constitutes the novel's emphasis on multiplicity is the Ruler—an assemblage of multiple historical figures. As a figure, the Ruler stands in for the African reification and internalization of Western practices of colonial modernity. The Ruler's liberal ideology of sovereignty, autonomy, self-making, and individualism represents the main identifications that constitute Western Enlightenment modernity, also known as colonial modernity, a naming that acknowledges the "twinned flourishing of liberal modernity and modern colonialism" (Shepard 19). In *Something Torn and New*, Ngũgĩ's non-fiction work that also explores the cultural effects of colonialism and globalization, he argues that the European Enlightenment, capitalist modernity, and colonialism cannot be separated from one another (xi). He writes, "There is no region, no culture, no nation today that has not been affected by colonialism and its aftermath. Indeed, modernity can be considered a product of colonialism" (xi). Ngũgĩ's linking of the Enlightenment, modernity, and colonialism underscores the tension inherent in tenets of Enlightenment ideology, such as the belief in the unequivocal good of development alongside the devastatingly uneven effects of the material practices that constitute such development, such as colonialism and contemporary economic processes of globalization, neo-liberalism and neo-colonialism. *Globalization*, *neo-liberalism* and *neo-colonialism* broadly refer to exploitative relations that are created by hierarchical rather than equitable integration into the global capitalist market economy. Such integration often occurs through the infrastructure, institutions, and ideological assumptions of colonialism, which function to keep wealth flowing from former colonies to former colonial powers (Stiglitz). In his article "Globalism's Discontents," economist and Nobel Laureate Joseph Stiglitz attributes "the most adverse effects" of globalization to "the liberalization of financial and capital markets" (A18). He argues that, as an economic ideology, market liberalization functions "as a new form of the old colonial mentality" (A18). Theorist Achille

Mbembe argues that the heart of "European colonial humanism" lies in its "procedures for racializing the colonized" ("What Is Postcolonial Thinking?). As such, some of the most devastating effects of these economic, ideological, and philosophic discourses are their racializing effects—their production of an African difference that justifies the inequalities of modern economic, cultural, and political structures; contemporary post-colonial white supremacy and nationalism; and anti-Blackness.

The Ruler, as a figure educated in colonial schools and who "came into power with flaming swords, the bodies of his victims falling down to his left and right like banana trunks," stands in for the brute position of Western colonial modernity and its reification of sovereignty, the nation state, and whiteness (Ngũgĩ, *Wizard* 10). Again, using the strategy of literalizing and concretizing an ideological position by rendering it materially, Ngũgĩ turns the stripes on the Ruler's suit into explicit markers of the bruteness of contemporary ruling elites. He writes,

> on careful examination one could see that the stripes were made of tiny letters that read MIGHT IS RIGHT. Rumor had it that all his clothes were made to measure in Europe, that his London, Paris, and Rome tailors did nothing else but make his clothes. What distinguished his clothes from all imitations by all political fawns were the patches on the shoulders and elbows of the jackets, because they were made from skins of the big cats, mainly leopards, tigers, and lions. In short, no politician was allowed to wear clothes with patches from the skins of His Mighty Cats. (19–20)

The stripes become a symbol for the way African elites have internationalized the values that drove colonial expansion, which cohere around the principle that physical power constitutes ethical imperative. In this image, animal skins, which are again used as stereotypical signifiers of Africa, become decorative marks that confirm African difference by augmenting the superior value of whiteness as figured by the European-tailored suits. The key racializing effect of positioning whiteness as superior affects the subject positions available in modernity. So Ngũgĩ's call for decolonization encompasses transformation of economic, psychic, and epistemic realities in order to achieve liberatory modes of consciousness.

The aesthetics of *Wizard of the Crow* work in opposition to values in Western Enlightenment modernity: its privileging of the nation-state as the primary spatial configuration of belonging; its privileging of autonomous, individual subjects; and its privileging of whiteness. Ngũgĩ's representational strategies privilege multiplicity in order to decenter the normative effect of the imperial imaginary. His representational strategies reveal the absurdity of the epistemology of whiteness espoused by both the West and postcolonial native elites. The primary representtational strategy used in the novel to foreground multiplicity is its deployment of heteroglossia in the sense of presenting a diversity of voices that differ from the official national narrative to trouble the idea that "the Ruler was the sole voice of the people" (24); and, more important, to trouble the very notion that the postcolonial nation can be narrated with one coherent narrative. The multiple modes of address in the narration—song snippets, hymns, lines from poems, Arabic verse, dances, folk wisdom, popular sayings, proverbs, rumors, newspaper headlines and articles, fantastic interludes, messianic registers, and satiric and ironic modes—work in opposition to the imperial imaginary by privileging multiple modes of knowledge to transcend Western modes of rationality and grand narratives of truth. Ngũgĩ uses the speculative genre as a tool for epistemic decolonization by positioning dance, song, performance, and fantasy as modes of truth in the same way that rationality is. Cultural production as performance becomes one of the chief ways that *Wizard of the Crow* represents oppositional consciousness. For example, young people in the novel create a performative mode of belonging after the Ruler learns of an insurgent group called the Voice of the People, linking performativity to modes of resistance. This group plants plastic snakes at the Ruler's compulsory birthday and start a riot. In response, the Ruler goes on TV to re-establish his authority over all things seen and unseen. Ngũgĩ writes,

> In biblical times, it was the Mosaic snakes that swallowed the Pharaonic ones. Today in Aburĩria, it is the Pharaonic snakes that will swallow all of you who think that you are the new Moses.
>
> And suddenly he raised the club higher in the air as if ready to throw it at any self-styled Moseses. The cameramen ducked behind their cameras, and all at once, as if hit by the same object simultaneously, every television screen in the country split into seven pieces. The viewers did not know whether the Ruler had actually thrown the club or simply had the power of mind to disintegrate their screens; disagreements remain to this day. Whatever the truth, the television performance did inspire a new snake dance, which became all the rage so that whenever and wherever two or three young people met, they would move their bodies—heads, torso, and hands—in serpentine motions as they sang:
>
> *The pot I made is broken*
> *Little did I know that freedom*

*Would bear a viper and a devil* (25)

This performative, inventive song created by the young people suggests critique of power and more expansive modes of belonging through the biblical references to Moses, who led the Jewish exodus out of Egypt. In this way, Ngũgĩ brings the thematic resonance of diaspora into play.

In addition, the plastic snakes as tools to incite protest and the snake dance as a performance of protest transforms or re-values the symbolic resonance of the serpent as an archetypal figure. In the Bible, the serpent is a figure of deceit that entices Eve to eat from "the tree of knowledge of good and evil" (Genesis 2:9). Ngũgĩ plays on this subversive meaning of the serpent to create a symbolic vocabulary for the very movements of protest to absolute power and the development of oppose-tional consciousness and practices in the novel, again trans-forming the symbolic and epistemic economies that undergird postcolonial modernity. The snake song itself captures the essence of the ambivalence of the postcolonial nation—how its promise of freedom remains unachieved. By imagining national-ism as the specific form that anti-colonial struggle would take, postcoloniality reproduces "the very logic of Enlightenment" (Gikandi 630). In this way, postcoloniality is engaged with the central problematic of modernity—perhaps a central proble-matic of earlier epochs as well: How does one achieve freedom? Given the articulation of the ambivalent nature of sovereignty—the way that it exposes one to the freedom of agency as well as to the risk of domination and oppression—with the desire for sovereignty that drives the postcolonial, postcoloniality is haunted by "the impossibility of getting over and done" with colonial modernity, always "running the risk of repeating it and perpetuating it" (Mbembe 1). Ngũgĩ casts multiplicity and difference into this cycle of the endless reproduction of the same in the service of the creation of oppositional consciousness.

Such a privileging of multiplicity affirms Third World feminist epistemologies and theories about oppositional modes of subjectivity. Third World, or transnational, feminist theory developed out of the recognition of the role that traditional feminism played in European colonization. Traditional, or Euro-American feminism supported hierarchal divisions within the category "woman" based on white supremacy and the construction of racial difference. Third World feminist Chandra Mohanty writes,

> [Oppositional consciousness] is a plural consciousness in that it requires understanding multiple, often opposing ideas and knowledges, and negotiating these knowledges, not just taking a counterstance. ... This notion of the uprooting of dualistic thinking suggests a conceptualization of consciousness, power, and authority that is fundamentally based on knowledges that are often contradictory. (80–81)

Narration—the self-conscious rendering of story as unstable representation rather than truth—is the primary trope that drives the aesthetics of multiplicity in novel. The novel begins, "There were many theories about the strange illness of the second Ruler of the Free Republic of Aburĩria, but the most frequent on people's lips were five" (3). The opening line binds together images of illness, republicanism, and narration. This assemblage of concerns taken up by the opening image stitches the primary concerns of modernity—sovereignty and the nation-state—to notions of ambiguity, instability, and disease. In this way, the novel deploys multiplicity to talk about how the ideologies of Western modernity play out differently in post-colonial contexts. By beginning with the multiple stories of illness of the Ruler, Ngũgĩ frames his novel as a retelling, or assemblage, of many different story fragments, just as the Ruler is an assemblage of many different historical figures. Constantly putting difference and ambiguity into play in this satirical, speculative representation of African postcoloniality suggests that, instead of being an unequivocal experience of freedom, decolonization is an uneven experience traversed by class and gender, to name just two lines of fragmentation. In other words, the experience of freedom is mediated through multiple modes of representing and narrating power.

## NARRATING THE NOW AND THE NOT-YET

> She told them that the only grace they could have
> was the grace they could imagine.
> –Toni Morrison
> (*Beloved* 88)

The novel's narration and representational strategies suggest this profound sense of fragmentation and difference in experiences of postcoloniality. The figure of the Ruler stands in as the mode of postcolonial power that imagines itself an imperial power "in the manner of the lords of old Europe" (6), a mode of power that impinges upon possibilities for, and experiences of, freedom. While power affords experiences of freedom for some, imperial power freezes time for others, offering no possibilities of freedom. In its ability to affect the future, this impingement shapes the uneven temporality of postcoloniality—what Bhabha calls "a double temporality": a process of coming into being that is punctuated by the gap between the production of desire and its fulfillment (in Fanon xvii). The gap between an idea and its expression. The gap between experience and representation. The gap between infection and apex of the surge. The present gap between the hopes for decolonization and the experience of its current representations, practices, performances, and subject positions in postcolonial African societies and within post-coloniality more broadly. Or, as the ruler thinks to himself before he freezes Rachael's present, "There is always a difference between a thought and its description" (7). While contemporary globalization theory often focuses on spatial representations and the uninterrupted flow of capital, Ngũgĩ represents both the temporal flows and stoppages of postcoloniality. Ngũgĩ puts us right in the gap, puts us inside difference. As a mode of narration, satire exposes the difference between how things are and how they should, or could, be—as does decolonization as a project.

As a mode of self-constituting desire, decolonization is a kind of gap. This gap is articulated through the iterative processes of revaluing, resignification, and reproduction, producing the effect of the multiple temporalities of the now, the then, and the not yet that constantly call the production of a finally pinned-down desire into question. In other words, any particular desire can be recalled and reconfigured by articulating a new relationship between the past, the present, and the future—something the speculative genre does well. In his work on Afrofuturism, literary theorist Justin Izzo identifies the decolonizing work of the speculative genre in the way it positions the reader. Speculative techniques create a "mirror-effect" by allowing the reader to compare the imaginative cartography to the real world, in particular to a real world that produces Black inferiority through epistemic frameworks and institutional practices, creating a mediated conversation between "the 'real' present of the reader who confronts the mirror-image of his or her world in the text" (186, 188). Ngũgĩ uses the speculative genre to reveal "the reifying assumptions and ideological contradictions underpinning the history of Western perceptions of Africa," to satirize "the history claims that Western knowledge makes about Africa," and to position the reader to re-value contemporary symbolic, epistemic, and psychic imaginaries (Izzo 186).

Through its genre and its central conceit of five stories of the Ruler's illness that drive the action forward, *Wizard of the Crow's* trajectory of recalling and reworking serves as a re-membering of the postcolonial imaginary—as site of contestation, a site of decolonization. This constant contingency of mediation, contestation, and reworking that the project of decolonization entails can reflect, but can also challenge, the repetition of the same values of colonial modernity. In addition, by constantly foregrounding mediation, the central conceit of the novel—the circulation of the many rumors of the Ruler's illness—works to underscore the temporal effects of narration. Ngũgĩ's novel demonstrates the radically transformative power of storytelling by exposing the diverse mediation effects of narration. In this way, the symbolic economy of the novel introduces what Bhabha calls "a temporal dimension into the discourse of decolonization" that works against "the *spatial* imagination . . . [of] geopolitical thinking" (in Fanon xiv). This shift away from decolonization as a spatial concept allows for imaginaries of belonging outside of the nation state. Ultimately, by staging narration as a site of anti-colonial resistance, Ngũgĩ suggests that the project of decolonization is "imaginable" and "achievable" (in Fanon xiv).

In this way, Ngũgĩ's representational strategies—including the multiple modes of address in the novel, its focus on performance, its genre, and its use literalizing metaphors—work in service of the fundamental Third World feminist value to "foreground questions of memory, experience, knowledge, history, consciousness, and agency in the creation of narratives of the (collective) self" (Mohanty 82). Through these represent-tational strategies, Ngũgĩ positions writing as fundamental to creating oppositional consciousness in the way that narration, as representation, can resist and transform previous codings of value by reworking understandings of the past, present, and future. The connection between writing, memory, and the oppositional subjectivity necessary to achieve decolonization is a prominent theme in contemporary theory. In *Feminism without Borders: Decolonizing Theory, Practicing Solidarity*, Mohanty articulates the Third World feminist understanding that political power is derived from developing viable oppositional alliances around common contexts of struggle, such as exploitative global socio-economic structures; such oppositional alliances can constitute diasporic Black belonging (49).

The deployment of diaspora through Ngũgĩ's allusional structure allows for an imaginary beyond the national as a form of belonging "generating desire for new kinds of identification" (Makokha). In the article "Migritude as a Cultural Spirit of Our Times," Justus Siboe Makokha argues that diaspora, as a new form of identification, offers

> a critique of discourses of fixed origins while taking account of a homing desire, as distinct from a desire for a homeland. … [It] is quests for those places where African people *will feel at home* that really lead to the "homing desire" epitomized by … [the] invitation to expand the temporal and spatial dimensions of our narrations of African nations in the manner of Ngũgĩ's *Wizard of the Crow*.

Given Ngũgĩ's focus on diaspora and the uneven effects of the global market economy, the local and global serve as two colliding narrative registers that structure the text and structure the diasporic and transnational Black subjectivity that is represented as an effect of narration. In addition to these spatial registers, the speculative genre troubles the text's sense of reality, representing the social paradox/non-coherence of the lived experience of democracy outside of and in relation to U.S. borders—in other words, the way in which the institutions, values, and practices the United States as a democracy work to erode democracy and equity in Africa. The diverse mediation effects of narration—from the central tropes used, to the genre and narrative style—suggest that the literary is an effective mode to create the oppositional consciousness necessary to interrupt the anxious repetitions of colonial modernity in contemporary models of African postcoloniality—positioning art as a tool for transformation of postcoloniality writ large.

## WORKS CITED

Armah, Ayi Kwei. *Two Thousand Seasons.* Per Ankh, 1973.

Dinerstein, Joel. "Technology and Its Discontents: On the Verge of the Posthuman." *American Quarterly*, vol. 58, no. 3, 2006, pp. 569-595.

Dyer, Richard. *White: Essays on Race and Culture.* Routledge, 1997.

Eley, Geoff. "The Trouble with 'Race': Migrancy, Cultural Difference, and the Remaking of Europe." *After the Nazi Racial State: Difference and Democracy in Germany and Europe*, edited by Chin Rita, Heide Fehrenbach, Geoff Eley, and Atina Grossman, University of Michigan Press, pp. 137-182.

Fanon, Frantz. *The Wretched of the Earth: The Handbook for the Black Revolution That Is Changing the Shape of the World.* Grove Press, 1963.

Gikandi, Simon. "Globalization and the Claim of Postcoloniality." *South Atlantic Quarterly*, vol. 100, 2001, pp. 627-658.

Izzo, Justin. "Historical Reversibility as Ethnographic Afrofuturism: Abdourahman Waberi's Alternative Africa." *Paradoxa: The Futures Industry*, vol. 27, pp. 183-204, paradoxa.com/volumes/27.

Lovesey, Oliver. "Ngũgĩ wa Thiong'o's Postnation: The Cultural Geographies of Colonial, Neocolonial, and Postnational Space." *MFS Modern Fiction Studies*, vol. 48, no. 1, Spring 2002.

Makokha, Justus Siboe. "Migritude as Cultural Spirit of Our Times." *Shailja Patel*, June 30, 2007, http://shailja.com/news/newsletterblog/2007/06/migritude-as-cultural-spirit-of-our.html.

Mbembe, Achille. *On the Postcolony.* University of California Press, 2001.

Mohanty, Chandra. *Feminism without Borders: Decolonizing Theory, Practicing Solidarity.* Duke University Press, 2003.

Mongin, Olivier Mongin, Lempereur, Nathalie Lempereur and Schlegel, Jean–Louis Schlegel. "What Is Postcolonial Thinking?" Translated by John Fletcher, *Eurozine*, 9 Jan. 2008, www.eurozine.com/articles/2008-01-09-mbembe-en.html.

Morrison, Toni. *Beloved.* Vintage, 2004.

Ngũgĩ wa Thiong'o. *Wizard of the Crow.* First Anchor Books, 2006.

———. *Decolonising the Mind.* James Curry Ltd., 1986.

———. *Something Torn and New: An African Renaissance.* Basic*Civitas* Books, 2009.

Nussbaum, Martha. *Love's Knowledge: Essays on Philosophy and Literature.* Oxford University Press, 1992.

Pozo, Michael. "An Interview with Ngũgĩ Wa Thiong'o." *St. John's University Humanities Review*, vol. 2, no. 2, May 2004, http://facpub.stjohns.edu/~ganterg/sjureview/vol2-2/05Pozo-Thiong.htm.

"Review of *Wizard of the Crow.*" *Kirkus Reviews*, vol. 74, no. 24, Special

Section, 15 Dec. 2006, p. 16., http://proxy.lib.uiowa.edu/login?url=http://search.ebscohost.com/login.aspx?direct=true&AuthT=ip,cookie,uid,url&db=afh&AN=23570162&loginpage=Login.asp&site=ehost-live.

Shepard, Todd. "Muslim French Citizens in Algeria." *The Invention of Decolonization: The Algerian War and the Remaking of France*. Cornell University Press, 2006, pp. 19–55.

Stiglitz, Joseph E. "Globalism's Discontents." *The American Prospect: Globalism and the World's Poor*, 5 Jan. 2002, https://prospect.org/features/globalism-s-discontents.

Stoler, Ann. "Tense and Tender Ties: The Politics of Comparison in North American History and (Post) Colonial Studies." *The Journal of American History*, 2001, pp. 829–865.

Sulaiman, Tosin. "Ngũgĩ's Remembrance of Things Past." *234Next.com*, 2010, http://234next.com/csp/cms/sites/Next/ArtsandCulture/Books/5538496-147/story.csp.

Wallerstein, I. "The Rise and Future Demise of the World Capitalist System: Concepts for Comparative Analysis." *The Capitalist World-Economy*, Cambridge University Press, 1979, pp. 1–14, http://catdir.loc.gov/catdir/samples/cam034/ 78002955.pdf.

Wildenthal, Lora. *German Women for Empire, 1884–1945*. Duke University Press, 2001.

# AMERICAN ANGER, HEARTS OF DARKNESS, AND *THE RADIANCE OF THE KING*: WHY CLARENCE MIGHT BE OUR GUY

Robert Helgeson

American culture is fractured. It doesn't take much to discern this. Whether bifurcated along a blue-red fissure or shattered into a million political, religious, ethnic, economic pieces, the land of *e pluribus unum* is currently a house divided and maybe even subdivided. Sadly, the divisions are both intense and ominous, fueled by "true believers" who see anyone not in their ranks as a rank offense to traditional American values, progressive values, human decency, and/or common sense. Street protests and Capitol violence have both embodied and epitomized a scorched emotional and ideological state of affairs that a society claiming to be one nation cannot long sustain.

So, what obtains?

With a polarized populace, what obtains is not merely a difference of opinion, but profound disagreements that seem to defy reasonable discussion. Matt Taibbi has thoughts on the matter. He lays much of the blame for this atomization at the feet of mass media and social media. To read his *Hate, Inc.* is to take the pulse of media in the throes of a fever dream of profits. Once based on a model of centrist positions and civility as means for reaching the broadest possible market, the media have exchanged the old strategy for a new economic model based on building up lucrative niche markets fueled by extreme views, extreme loyalty, and strident voices. The new media model focuses on a tribalist drive for profits by catering to fear and aggression.

According to a recent op-ed by Charlie Warzel in *The New York Times*, Michael Goldhaber, a theoretical physicist whom Warzel calls "The Cassandra of the Internet Age," anticipated as much in a 1997 essay published in *Wired* magazine in which he first posited his notion of "the attention economy." Commenting on the rise and likely impact of the Internet, he was among the first to describe attention as a commodity that increasingly would be in demand. He asserted that profits in such an economy primarily would go to those who could capture and command attention as long as possible and convert that attention into consumeristic activity. Among his observations was that the most extreme views or opinions generally garnered the most attention and that the doyens of this brave new world could maximize their profits by creating a crisis mentality that compelled people to pay attention. The truth of this is easily observable by watching nightly weather reports where threatened storms routinely take on ominous potential. This state of readiness and fear sown among the populace is not unlike that demanded by an unending "War on Terror" that benefits its own range of opportunistic industries.

One result of this shift in the media's economic model is that "mainstream" media gave way to clearly biased mastheads, stations, and networks, while moderates morphed into the Rush Limbaughs, Sean Hannities, and Rachel Maddows of the world, ersatz journalists whose essential talents seem to be conjuring bile, marshaling misinformation, spouting truisms rather than truth, and arranging carefully curated pundits to create programming marginally more serious than a run-of-the-mill teen influencer blog.

The result of this media climate, in short, is a culture starved of cogency, prodded by inaccuracy, energized by emotion, and characterized by a constant state of anxiety. Taibbi further suggests that modern media shape things to fit a sports template in which all conflict is binary and contested between adversaries with a playoff, win-at-all-costs mentality. In this context, anyone holding a divergent view is the enemy who must be neutralized in a zero-sum game. There is no room for a Venn diagram overlap, no basis for a discussion of shared interests. If Taibbi is even partially correct, is it a wonder that discourse exists at all? Stridency trumps civility every time.

Bari Weiss, an opinion writer whose name certainly generates a diversity of reactions, wrote recently of the "colonial" mindset that is now endemic to American culture. By this term she suggests that leading opinions tend to be produced by charismatic individuals or organized groups and imposed on the masses.

Similarly, Megan McArdle warned in a recent *Washington Post* op-ed of the corrosive effects of Twitter, describing the silos of cultural opinion, both left and right, around whose central tenets attenuated "facts" and pumped-up feelings swirl like poisoned eddies in the ocean of events. Odysseus himself might have difficulty steering safe passage.

Overall, the effect is to create communities of anger, says McArdle, in which "people try to make themselves safer through preemptive revenge … or take refuge in communities of extremists who will at least protect them from anyone on the other side, no matter what they say, as long as it is sufficiently far left or right." She continues,

> In exchange, of course, they demand that you smile tolerantly at the worst your own side can dish out. And that "worst" keeps getting worse because of a phenomenon well known to social scientists: when you sort

> people into ideological groups, the pressure of group-think tends to push both the groups themselves, and the people within them, to become more extreme than they were before.

So, as Sonny and Cher presciently crooned, "The beat goes on."

Well, what is to be done?

Decades ago Chinua Achebe famously criticized Joseph Conrad's *The Heart of Darkness* for its portrayal of Africa and African culture as chaotic and savage. Defenders of Conrad's novella argued that Achebe had missed the point, that the story was primarily focused on Mister Kurtz, the overlord whose European rational mindset, absent the strictures of western tradition—whether in Africa, Asia, or some other distinctly non-western locale—had gone crazy. Achebe, however, chose to see Kurtz not as crazy, but as arrogant and cruel. Kurtz was emblematic of a presumptuous colonial aggression that brazenly assumed an agenda of commercialism. Kurtz's job wasn't to understand Africa; it was to exploit Africa, and he was good at it because he had lost all sense of guilt.

Again, defenders of Conrad argued that the novella was meant to focus on the insanity of Kurtz and the dwindling sanity of Marlow as he felt himself "going native." Achebe had none of it. He saw the best minds of his culture ridiculously debased in *The Heart of Darkness* and other western literature. For that reason he devoted the opening two thirds of his novel *Things Fall Apart* to a realistic, almost sociological depiction of Okonkwo and his Ibo culture. When the district commissioner can muster only a paragraph to account for Okonkwo at the end of his novel, Achebe makes it clear that British colonial rule really had no clue as to what it was destroying. (A reading of *King Leopold's*

*Ghost* should suffice to identify the truly dark heart inhabiting Africa.) Achebe asserted that Conrad's narrative betrayed an entirely unrealistic vision of African culture. In Conrad's (and Europe's) view, African culture wasn't just different; it was different in scary, unpredictable, unfathomable ways. Confronted by this, Kurtz, as the colonial power, had no choice but to brutally subjugate or to annihilate the brutes.

A healthier attitude was that of British anthropologist Kenneth Murray, according to Nigerian artist Ben Onwonwu. Rather than promulgate a western conception of art among his African students, Murray encouraged a celebration of Indigenous traditions as well as the cultivation of a new African art.

*The Heart of Darkness*, of course, was only one of many distorted western depictions of Africa. These ranged from the cartoonish Tarzan, the white interloper who gave definition and relevance to the place simply by being plunked down in its midst, like a Christ child born into an African manger, to the romanticized *Out of Africa*, penned by Karen Blixen to affirm that no one could appreciate the continent as much as she, not even its native inhabitants who "surely lacked" the aesthetic, emotional, and spiritual capacity to do so.

Many African writers took pen in hand to reject such falsified histories and images. The aforementioned *Things Fall Apart* is perhaps the most well-known of these, but perhaps more revealing was the 1954 masterpiece, *The Radiance of the King*, written by Camara Laye. The protagonist of Laye's novel is a bedraggled and penniless colonial European, named Clarence, who wants to go home after the change of regimes. Still full of pretensions, he intends to confront the African king and demand sufficient payment to effect that return. Mere steps away from the king early in the story, he finds himself swept away on a journey bordering on magical realism, during which he is frustrated time and again from actually speaking with the king. He is rebuffed by crowds of people, by circumstances, by topography. And each leg of the journey leaves him more fatigued and vulnerable. Yet he is preserved by the kindness of the natives, engaged by their traditions and commerce, and captivated by the beauty of the people and their surroundings. Only when fully stripped of his pretensions and humbled by the goodness that has confronted and confounded him does Clarence finally gain access to the king. Only when his arrogance ebbs, his fortunes having turned on the kindness of those over whom he had ignorantly lorded, only when circumstances bring him to an educated and heartfelt humility does the path ultimately clear and allow him to address the king, a beautiful boy who, in a gesture of openness and generosity, parts his robe to reveal a heart of transcendent radiance. As T. S. Eliot might conclude, Mistah Kurtz, he dead. The west, far from the home of civility, had been overrun by hollow men. And the heart of Africa, too long denigrated as dark, is celebrated as resplendent.

The pilgrim in Dante's *Inferno* confesses in the opening canto of the epic poem that midway through his journey in life he found himself lost in a dark wood. Perhaps as fearful as was Clarence in a foreign land or Marlow going up the Congo River, Dante's pilgrim eagerly searches for respite or rescue. Before long he sees a sunlit hilltop emerging above the dark wood that he presumes will offer both. However, similar to Clarence, he finds his progress toward "salvation" blocked, in this case by three beasts representing his own "sinful" nature. Of course, what follows is his well-known trip through hell, eventually leading him to purgatory and ultimately to heaven. Dante, like Clarence, discovers that the path to redemption is not easy, obscured and blocked at many turns by his own obdurate pride. Only by means of the long journey, the arduous but enlightening undertaking from circle to circle, sin to sin, and horrible outcome to horrible outcome does Dante the pilgrim come to terms with the world as it is and his own fallen state. Stripped of his pretensions of holiness, Dante discovers the grace of a heart purified. . . as had Clarence.

A colonial arrogance undergirds the extremes of our current political/cultural right and left in America. Both assume airs based on an unsupported, unwarranted sense of rectitude. Insurrectionists storm the Capitol to save the nation. Progressives cleanse the libraries, museums, and public squares of provincial, parochial, or unenlightened works of art to save the minds of students and children. The exercises of power in the name of either bear the same appearance of Kurtz's militant malignancy—smug, pompous, and essentially cruel. Intolerance masquerades as progressiveness. Privilege marches in formation as patriotism. Dialogue is slatterned to diatribe. The swagger of extremity is goaded on by media and social media blowhards whose capacity for empathy, sympathetic understanding, or simple grace lies stillborn.

One possible solution to the situation might be to hop in a truck called Rosinante like John Steinbeck and travel across America, open-hearted and sticking to the "blue highways" while listening for the "hillbilly elegy," and welcoming the least among us.

In his landmark 2011 book, *The Righteous Mind*, Jonathan Haidt suggests that most people want to be good. In what is now popularly termed "moral foundations theory," Haidt argues that the vast majority of people want to be "moral." He suggests that people create their fundamental sense of morality from combinations of six primary factors: care versus harm, fairness versus cheating, loyalty versus betrayal, respect for authority versus subversion, sanctity versus degradation, and liberty versus oppression. He explains some of the current social roiling by suggesting that groups create their unique sense of right and wrong by establishing their moral foundation based on different hierarchies of the six factors. For some, respect for authority is paramount while, for others, liberty is the key even at the expense of loyalty. For yet others, caring and fairness are the most essential and respect for authority is only a minor consideration. What emerges according to Haidt are different notions of what constitutes "good." While people on the whole want to be good, the disagreement on what constitutes "good," when framed and touted by profit-seeking media and social-media influencers, is problematic.

Camara Laye saw what the colonial mind was capable of perpetrating. Modern America suffers under the hand of its own colonial masters. Kurtz-like zealots have run amok, and measure goodness by their own parochial pride, and govern or "cancel" according to impossible standards of tribal purity in displays of singular arrogance. Laye and Dante both attest that arrogance is mitigated only by humility, and the fruit of humility is grace. In an environment where the idea of diversity too often is used to sow division rather than as an impetus for finding common humanity; where the "cloistered virtue" of identity-based self-interest replaces ideals of common ground and common good; where people nurse hurt pride rather than seeking reconciliation, there is a lot of work to be done. We have to break a sweat if we hope to break down the walls of enmity.

There is no quick and easy approach to the king, no short cut up the hill into the radiant sunlight. Achebe's district commissioner cannot explain in a paragraph the life of Okonkwo or the culture that he defended. Understanding takes time. It takes effort. It takes watching and listening and learning. In America, we have a way to go.

## WORKS CITED

Haidt, Jonathan. *The Righteous Mind: Why Good People Are Divided by Politics and Religion*. Vintage, 2013.

Laye, Camara. The Radiance of the King.

McArdle, Megan. "Opinion: It's time for major institutions to make their employees get off of Twitter." *Washington Post*, 22 Jan. 2021, www.washingtonpost.com/opinions/2021/01/22/its-time-major-institutions-make-their-employees-get-off-twitter.

Taibbi, Matt. *Hate, Inc.* OR Books, 2019.

Warzel, Charlie. "I Talked to the Cassandra of the Internet Age." *New York Times*, 4 Feb. 2021, www.nytimes.com/2021/02/04/opinion/michael-goldhaber-internet.html.

# PARROT

*For Peter*

Returning to Greece, Alexander brought a bird
"speaking an Indian language" – Aristotle recording
in animal history and Ctesias notes—for a thousand

Years Europe thinking parrots only came from India

You held that stick passing it back and forth Moira
Kololo Makerere Leeds—Yorkshire man Boycott
white buttoned down flannels driving elegantly

Through covers brown hands catching red
sphere stitched leather disrupted and willowed
to Boundaries: raven, or was that crow, exulting

I have the longest memory—Ganesh elephant-headed—
I perch on ledges webbed on swamp-cypress limbs
I shall remember you to yourselves returning voices

Konkani—Jazz in Africa Armstrong blowing life breath
into adopted saxophone fingers and lips vibrating
prana and curiosity—opening that bag—no slumber

Odysseus, fire-engine sirens waking neighbourhood
disrupting old orders in a pandemic—I did I didn't
come from Wuhan I did not come from labs I did

Not come from pangolins—bat stroking sphere
gliding on clipped green to boundary not baseball
not cricket not tiger putting on grass or putting gas

Into endless tanks not wind in sails in Dutch blades
now metalled in China or Spain Don Quixote charging

I ride an ass I am Sancho faithful companion follower

Astride a donkey I wear a thorn crown
plasma leaking unto forehead into eyes—what
has been as simple as a falcon's dive lord

Of birds fastest terrestrial creature clocking 242 mph
not kilometers but Roman measure not cheetah's
burst on savannah bringing down wildebeest or deer

Big cat brave-hearted lion—singha—leaping
to East Africa or Southeastern Asia Malaysia Singa-
pore's neither man nor beast Merlion crossing oceans

Ulysses Sanskritized Irish English words running
unto another word another line page breath, Bharat's
ancient treatise on dance music rhythm in mouth feet

Shiva unlost in Kampala, heads feeding fishes—what!
we haven't renamed a Lake Victoria—imperial
utterance we brandish with love grain-hoarder-Caliban

White-crowned George rising at York—"my hair
is grey, but not with years, nor grew it white
in a single night"—*ah O twist karay dam da da*

*da da da dam, ah O twist karay*—Junglee Kapoor
in Mumbai imitating Elvis vinyl spinning areas
of darkness engulfing America—watch your part

of speech your tense your dissent your prepositions
odd in New England snow falling on Yale on Boston
harbour insurrection against old King George

China tea or Darjeeling's dumped overboard, native
tribes taking sides red-coated cardinal welcoming
dawn on paling blue jay screaming—you still hold

Colonial colours—republican red mimicry British military
blue democrat a default French smarting Drake
victories or Hawkins'—blue privateers blue Fleur-de-lis

Fluttering in Florida on Quebecois antennas Atlantic
waters down middle passages tending to equinoxes
Japanese by spring another trickster from Africa

Spiders inhabiting landmasses in trickster traditions
the land is everything—story and character—Geronimo
finally subdued transported two thousand miles

To St Augustine to a Spanish citadel unvanquished
vanquished in a dark cell converted to Christ
ocean roaring in ears far from Chihuahua-Sonora sands

Straddling what U.S.—Mexican border ancestral grounds
unboundaried plains—Wounded Knee Little Big Horn
echoing over tall grass concealing bunting cougar peregrine

Falcon diving blood cardinal calls lighting dawn tweets
on Mediterranean fruit Florida-ized machine gunned beaking
woodpecker targeting dried Indian orchid bark—I bloom

Anywhere in the fall, give me a little cold or snow
Iowa or Alberta how—did you arrive from Yale or London
Salvam Salwan Selvan Selvon or Nazareth ancestral

Name in Goan gumbo garam masala Mississippi masala
Kampala masala Amin up general up moon up

Your time up Indian—no, not you with no name
no fleecing Indian name—keeping my finances under
poetry under Eliot or some biblical passage clothed

In a brown mantle Islam or Judaism still people
of the book not Patels or Bengali babus Bhagchee

Mukherjee Dutt Blaze Narayan Narayan Narayan

Narareth a brown thrasher skimming hedge beyond fence
a spring arrivant Holi-splashed African orchids blooming
somewhere in Moira—Prabhu a Konkani gift my name

In banana fronds in beaks of birds keepers and markers
of land and music notating a Rigveda or Yajurveda's verse
only bird "uttering human speech"—songs parrot ragas

Sasenarine Persaud

## A WRITER

*Tribute to Peter Nazareth*

Exposing and archiving,
The complex ideas and thoughts of
Humanity's kaleidoscopic song.

Documenting stories and notes,
Memos and meetings; mentoring.
Building families, empowering communities.

Looping, weaving, singing,
Our distinct and interconnected stories, songs.

Creating our multi-layered truths,
Supporter and promoter;

Fashioning needed space and places.

Embracing our chosen identities.
Cultivator, celebrator
Of that deep voice within.

Rooted,

In the ancient legacy of the word.

Joseph K. Henry

# CONTRIBUTORS

RAQUEL BAKER earned a PhD in English Literary Studies from the University of Iowa. She specializes in Postcolonial Studies and $20^{th-}$ and $21^{st}$-century African literatures in English. She received a BA in Psychology from San Francisco State University and an MFA in Creative Writing from Mills College. She is currently an Assistant Professor of Postcolonial and Transnational Literatures at California State University Channel Islands, where she teaches creative writing and contemporary African literature courses. In Spring 2021, she will be teaching "Reparations and Reconciliations," covering how art has been used in Indigenous truth, reconciliation, and reparations processes in Africa and the Americas.

JOSH BARKAN has won the Lightship International Short Story Prize and has been a finalist for the Grace Paley Prize for Short Fiction, the Paterson Fiction Prize, and the Juniper Prize for Fiction. He is the recipient of a fellowship from the National Endowment for the Arts, and his writing has appeared in Esquire. He earned his MFA from the Iowa Writers' Workshop and has taught writing at Harvard, Boston University, and New York University. His latest book, *Mexico*, was named one of the five Best Books of literature of 2017 by Library Journal.

SANDRA (SANDY) BARKAN studied French at Cornell University and UCLA. In London, where she studied in preparation for a trip to Uganda, she studied and briefly worked for the *New African* with the journal's literature editor, the South African writer Lewis Nkosi, laying the groundwork for her future study of African literatures. As a student in the African Studies graduate program at Makerere University she studied African literatures with David Cook, Peter Nazareth's professor at an earlier date. These experiences led her to teach African literatures at the University of California Irvine, the University of Iowa – where she also got her PhD in Comparative Literature – Middlebury College, Legon University in Ghana with Kofi Anyidoho, and the University of Cape Town in South Africa with Etienne van Heerden, both writers and academics with links to Iowa's International Writing Program. Barkan was also an administrator at the University of Iowa, including serving one year as the Interim Director of the International Writing Program. She was an active member of the African Literature Association, holding several offices including President, and served as Treasurer for the African Studies Association. After retiring from the University of Iowa, Barkan moved to Washington, DC, where she worked for the International Visitor Leadership Program, one of the Department of State's cultural diplomacy programs. She has once more retired.

AUSTIN BUKENYA is one of the pioneering African scholars of English and literature in East Africa. He taught for many years in Kenya.

NATAŠA ĎUROVIČOVÁ is the editor of the International Writing Program, affiliate faculty at the MFA in Literary Translation, both at the University of Iowa, and the co-editor of *World Cinemas, Transnational Perspectives* (2011) and *At Translation's Edge* (2019).

S. G. ELLERHOFF holds a PhD from the School of English at Trinity College Dublin. He is the author of *Mole* (Reaktion Books, 2020), *Post-Jungian Psychology and the Short Stories of Ray*

*Bradbury and Kurt Vonnegut* (Routledge, 2016), *Tales From the Internet* (Norbert Allen Books, 2015), and *Time's Laughingstocks* (Norbert Allen Books, 2013). He also co-edited *George Saunders: Critical Essays* (Palgrave Macmillan, 2017) and *Exploring the Horror of Supernatural Fiction: Ray Bradbury's Elliott Family* (Routledge, 2020). His most recent publication is "White Supremacy and the Multicultural Imagination in Ray Bradbury's Afrofuturist Stories of Mars" for the *Journal of Modern Literature.*

RASIAH HALIL is a poet, writer, translator and educator. Published since 1972, Rasiah's works dwell largely on social and humanitarian issues. Her books include *Perbualan Buku Catatan Seorang Gipsi (Conversations: Notebook of a Gypsy)* (1988), *Orang Luar (The Outsider)* (1991), *Sungai & Lautan (River & Ocean)* (1995), *Ayah Tidak Sayang Padaku Lagi (Father No Longer Loves Me)* (2007), *Hikayat Sri Anggerik (The Chronicles of Sri Anggerik)* (2007), and *Nyanyian Si Anak Dagang (Songs of the Outsider)* (2013), and her works can also be found in various compilations. Since 1983, Rasiah's works received a number of awards, including the Tun Seri Lanang Award. Under the pseudonyms of 'Sri Anggerik' and 'Tun Fatimah', Rasiah wrote topics on human interest and literature for *Berita Minggu* (Singapore Malay newspaper). Rasiah taught in Singapore and Brunei and attended the Iowa International Writing Program in 1995 on a Fulbright Scholarship.

ROBERT HELGESON, PHD, is a retired teacher. His career included stops at Marist Sisters College – Woolwich in Sydney, Australia, where he also participated in the New South Wales Higher School Certificate testing program; Hastings (MN) High School; and Apple Valley (MN) High School where he served several years as English Department Coordinator. He was active in curriculum development and assessment at the district and state levels, and participated in Advanced Placement training. He also was a four-term elected member of the Mounds View ISD 621 School Board. His love of contemporary African fiction, nurtured as it was by Professor Peter Nazareth, was reflected in all aspects of his educational career and served as the basis for a variety of presentations and publications.

JOSEPH K. HENRY is from St. Louis, Missouri, and he received his MA Degree from Boston University in Massachusetts. He currently serves as the Recruitment & Outreach Coordinator in the Office of Graduate Diversity, Equity, and Inclusion for the University of Iowa. His mission is to recruit, support, and help retain graduate student populations that have been historically underserved and underrepresented in higher education. Among his awards, he was recognized with The Contributing to Student Success Award at the first annual celebration of Black Scholarship, Leadership and Achievement that was hosted by the Society of Black Graduate and Professional Students in 2019. He also received the Black Lives Matter at School Award, sponsored by the Black Lives Matter at School Gala in Iowa City on February 7, 2020.

DANSON KAHYANA is a senior lecturer in the literature department at Makerere University, Uganda, and currently a Fulbright Research Fellow at the African Studies Centre, Michigan State University. Although he has not met Prof. Peter Nazareth in person, he has corresponded with him for ten years, and immensely benefited from his generosity. When Kahyana was writing his doctoral dissertation on Ugandan literature at Stellenbosch University, Prof. Nazareth was the unofficial third supervisor. For his Fulbright Research Fellowship, Kahyana was to be advised by Prof. Nazareth at the University of Iowa, but because of the disruptions caused by the Covid-19 pandemic, this was not to be.

SUSAN NALUGWA KIGULI is an academic and poet. She holds a PhD in English from the University of Leeds (UK) sponsored by the Commonwealth Scholarship Scheme. She is an Associate Professor in the Department of Literature, Makerere University. She was the African Studies Association Presidential Fellow, 2011 and this presented her with an opportunity to read her poetry at the Library of Congress, Washington, DC, in November 2011. She was a Poet in Residence at the Siftung Kunst: Raum Sylt Quelle, Germany between October- November 2008. She was also among three African poets who not only performed before the former President of Germany, His Excellency Horst Kohler in 2008 at the International Literature Festival Berlin, but was also honoured as one of the poets to appear in his book on Africa entitled *Schiskal Afrika* (2010). She has served as the chairperson of FEMRITE, Uganda Women Writers' Association. She currently serves on the Advisory Board for the African Writers Trust (AWT). She was the chief convener for both the 2nd Eastern African Literary & Cultural Studies Conference (August 2015) and Celebrating Ugandan Writing: Okot p'Bitek's *Song of Lawino* at 50 (March 2016), held at Makerere University, Uganda. She is the author of *The African Saga* and *Home Floats in a Distance/ Zuhause Treibt in der Ferne(Gedichte)*, a bilingual edition in English and German. She has recently participated in the Afro-women Poetry Project founded by the Italian journalist Antonella Sinopoli. Her research interests fall mainly in the area of oral and written African poetry, popular song, stylistics and performance theory. She writes poetry in both Luganda and English.

SUCHEN CHRISTINE LIM, awarded the Southeast Asia Write Award for her body of work, is the inaugural Singapore Literature Prize winner. Awarded a Fulbright grant, she is a Fellow in the University of Iowa's International Writing Program, and returned as the university's first Singapore Writer in Residence. A Fellow in Creative Writing at the Nanyang Technological University, Singapore, her novel *Fistful of Colours* is considered a classic Singapore novel, while her debut novel, *Rice Bowl*, is "a landmark novel on post-independence Singapore" and *The River's Song*, another novel, was selected by *Kirkus Reviews* (USA) as a "100 Best Books of 2015" and also Book of the Month in *The Sunday Times.*

BERNTH LINDFORS is Professor Emeritus of English and African Literatures at the University of Texas at Austin.

OLIVER LOVESEY is a Professor of English at the University of British Columbia, Okanagan, in Canada. He has written monographs on George Eliot, including most recently *Postcolonial George Eliot* (2017), and on Ngũgĩ wa Thiong'o, including most recently *The Postcolonial Intellectual: Ngũgĩ wa Thiong'o in Context* (2015). He edited *Approaches to Teaching the Works of Ngũgĩ wa Thiong'o* (2011) in the MLA's series and *Popular Music and the Postcolonial* (2019).

JULIE MARKUSSEN is a life-long lover of Elvis and a reality-tv junkie. Originally from Iowa, she now lives in California, where being a middle school administrator is her day job. On the weekends, you might find her visiting Elvis's Honeymoon Hideaway in Palm Springs or watching Girl Happy. She credits and thanks Peter Nazareth for helping her become a true Elvisologist.

DOM MARTIN was born in East Africa, and now lives in the USA; a gifted painter who exhibited his works in both India and the West, he is the author of *The Day Before the Day After*, *Exodus to Eternity*; *COEXISTENCE: Humanity's Wailing Wall*; *GENOCIDE: The New Order of Imperialism*, and *NAKBLINKA: The Cleansing of CoExistence*. See www.dommartin.us/

THOMAS MCCARTHY was born at Cappoquin, Co. Waterford, in 1954 and educated locally and at University College Cork. He is a member of *Aosdana*, the elected Assembly of artists and writers in Ireland. He was an Honorary Fellow of the *International Writing Program*, University of Iowa in 1978/79. He has published *The First Convention* (Dolmen Press, 1978), *The Sorrow Garden* (Anvil Poetry, 1981), *The Non-Aligned Storyteller* (Anvil Poetry, 1984), *Seven Winters in Paris* (Anvil Poetry, 1989), *Lost Province* (Anvil Poetry, 1996), *Merchant Prince* (Anvil Poetry, 2005) and *The Last Geraldine Officer* (Anvil Poetry, 2009), *Pandemonium* (Carcanet Press, 2016) and *Prophecy* (Carcanet Press, 2019). He has also published two novels, *Without Power* (Poolbeg, 1981) and *Asya and Christine* (Poolbeg, 1992) as well as two works of non-fiction, *Gardens of Remembrance* (New Island, 1996) and *Out of the Ashes* (Cork City Libraries, 2006). He has won the Patrick Kavanagh Award, the Alice Hunt Bartlett Prize, and the O'Shaughnessy Prize for Poetry, as well as the Ireland Funds *Annual Literary Award*. He worked for many years at Cork City Libraries, retiring in 2014 to write fulltime. He was International Professor of English at Macalester College, Minnesota, in 1994/95. He is a former Editor of *Poetry Ireland Review* and *The Cork Review*. His work is represented in more than thirty anthologies of Irish poetry, most notably in *Penguin Book of Irish Poetry* (2010), *Anthology of Irish Poetry* (Harvard University Press, 2013), *The Wake Forest Series of Irish Poetry: Volume II* (Wake

Forest University Press, 2010) and *Bitter Harvest* (Scribners, 1989).

CHRISTOPHER MERRILL has published seven collections of poetry, including *Watch Fire*, for which he received the Lavan Younger Poets Award from the Academy of American Poets; many edited volumes and translations; and six books of nonfiction, among them, *Only the Nails Remain: Scenes from the Balkan Wars*, *Things of the Hidden God: Journey to the Holy Mountain*, and *Self-Portrait with Dogwood.* His writings have been translated into nearly forty languages; his journalism appears widely; his honors include a Chevalier des Arts et des Lettres from the French government, numerous translation awards, and fellowships from the John Simon Guggenheim Memorial and Ingram Merrill Foundations. As director of the University of Iowa's International Writing Program since 2000, Merrill has conducted cultural diplomacy missions to more than fifty countries. He served on the U.S. National Commission for UNESCO from 2011-2018; in April 2012 President Barack Obama appointed him to the National Council on the Humanities.

ROCHELLE NAMEROFF was born in Wisconsin and holds degrees from U.C. Berkeley and the Iowa Writers Workshop. She teaches at California State University, East Bay. Her essays and poems have appeared in magazines including *The Iowa Review*, *The Michigan Quarterly Review*, *Antioch Review*, *Denver Quarterly*, *Seattle Review*, *Iowa Woman*, and many others. She still loves the Everly Brothers!

SASENARINE PERSAUD is the author of fourteen books of fiction and poetry and several essays on literature, politics and Indians in the Americas. His aesthetics, Yogic Realism, has been the subject of a PhD dissertation. Persaud's awards include The KM Hunter Foundation Award for Fiction (Toronto); the Arthur Schomburg Award (NY) for his contribution to Caribbean Literature; a Canada Council Award for Poetry; the Leslie Epstein Fellowship (Boston University); and the 2018 Dharmic Arts and Humanities Award from the Hindu American Foundation. Three decades of research into, and a lifelong engagement with, Indian philosophies and literature, yoga, art, languages and Indian classical music distinguishes his craft from his contemporaries. His work has been included in multiple anthologies, including the *Oxford Book of Caribbean Short Stories* and the *Oxford Book of Caribbean Verse*. *Monsoon on the Fingers of God* (2018) is his latest book.

JAMEELA SIDDIQI is an award-winning broadcaster, journalist, novelist, and a leading commentator on Indian classical music. She studied International History at the London School of Economics, after which she worked as a television news producer, scriptwriter and documentary director for several years while pursuing private studies in Indian classical dance and music and North Indian languages. She has translated film, folk and classical Indian poetry and songs and has acted as a language consultant for Oxford University Press whilst also contributing chapters to the *Routledge Encyclopaedia of Hinduism* and the *Penguin Rough Guide to World Music* (chapters on India and Pakistan) with a special focus on the devotional music of Hindus, Muslims and Sikhs, on which she has also written for *The Intimate Other – Love Divine in Indic Religions* (Longman Orient, 2005). Apart from writing, broadcasting (BBC Radio 3, Radio 4 & World Service), and lecturing extensively on all aspects of Indian classical music and culture, (including lectures at the annual Darbar Festival, London, and Raga on Strings, Cape Town) she has published two novels: *The Feast of the Nine Virgins*, 2001, and *Bombay Gardens*, 2006. She is the author of numerous short stories, essays and articles and is a regular reviewer and contributor for *Song-lines*, a leading journal of World Music. She has also taught on creative writing courses and acted as Course Manager and Lecturer for a degree course in North Indian Classical Music for Trinity-Laban and The Bhavan.

www.ingramcontent.com/pod-product-compliance
Lightning Source LLC
Chambersburg PA
CBHW062136160726
48282CB00027B/841
* 9 7 8 8 1 9 4 9 6 3 2 5 7 *